Water

Water Birds

Water Birds

Ranjit Lal

Rupa & Co

Copyright © Ranjit Lal 2006

Published 2006 by
Rupa & Co
7/16, Ansari Road, Daryaganj,
New Delhi 110 002

Sales Centres:

Allahabad Bangalore Chandigarh Chennai
Hyderabad Jaipur Kathmandu
Kolkata Mumbai Pune

Typeset in 12 AGaramond by
Nikita Overseas Pvt. Ltd.
1410 Chiranjiv Tower
43 Nehru Place
New Delhi 110 019

Printed in India by
Saurabh Printers Pvt. Ltd.
A-16 Sector-IV
Noida 201 301

Contents

Introduction

HAVE YOU EVER SAT BY THE EDGE OF A REED-FRINGED jheel or talao on a misty winter morning at dawn? If you get there early enough, when the sky is still dark purple and freckled with stars, and the waters are still and calm, snuggle into your windcheater and settle down. And listen...

A soft contented murmuring wafts over the water, interspersed with the occasional hoarse squawk—a throaty indignant *quaark*! Out there, on the velvety water there are ducks, feeding industriously and earnestly. Their murmuring conversation is soon drowned by querulous trumpeting notes drifting over from the middle of the lake. There, the cranes have begun to preen and straighten their feathers, and stretch their necks and legs, in preparation for take-off. As the sky lightens, you can just make out their droopy tailed silhouettes. One by one, single file, necks stretched out ahead, they begin to take- off like a squadron of bombers, but calling happily to each other now, in clear brassy trumpet-notes that lift your spirits up into the sky with them.

Soon, the sky is flushed peach-gold and the water, glinting pink and mauve at first, turns to molten lava. Effortlessly, the sun comes up, but as yet looking like a frosted orange straight from the freezer. Suddenly there is a commotion over the water—a great roar of beating wings and splashing flippers that makes your heart boom like a gigantic woofer. And suddenly there are what seems to be five thousand ducks all trying to take off at the same instant—rocketing, swirling, whirling everywhere. Somewhere in their midst, a hooded bandit—the marsh harrier—wings its way low and lazily. Its eyes will be on the water, its strange disc-like owl's face reflecting the sound of the faintest furtive sploosh straight to its ears. If there is a sick or straggling bird down there—it will have no chance to escape.

As calm returns and the ducks settle back, you spot a furtive sneaky movement in the reeds nearby. And hold your breath. A small, streaky brown heron is stalking slowly through the shallows, its yellow and black eyes rivetted to the water, its long scaly legs being lifted and lowered with an assassin's care. Suddenly the dagger bill flashes and there is a wriggling silver fish struggling at its end. With a dazzling flash of white wings, the heron flies off, swallowing the fish as it goes.

And all too soon you are wondering what to watch! Should you admire the beautiful golden caramel plumage of those brahminy ducks in the distance, or pay attention to those snazzy avocets still dozing in the water? Are those pelicans out there trying to organise themselves for a fishing expedition? And what are those teeming scuttling salt-and-pepper birds, with long legs and long bills, nipping this way and that in the mud? Ah, but here comes a cheery pied kingfisher and great, it has parked itself high above, hovering over the water, black dagger bill pointed straight down...and sploosh! And is that the murmur of geese you can hear? It sounds like people talking at a faraway party— but here they come, flying steadily, in formation, banking now, beautifully, and touching down. Back from having gorged themselves all night in some poor farmer's fields...

I'd better stop—I could go on and on all day. Watching water birds is like that. In this book you will meet just some of these spectacular creatures. You'll meet the 'waders', or what the Americans call, 'shorebirds': the big fellows like the storks and cranes and herons, and the little chaps like the sandpipers and plovers. (Be warned: some of these little fellows, the sandpipers for example, are all clad in very similar salt-and-pepper colours and can drive you nuts as you try to sort them out!) You'll meet several members of the great tribes of 'waterfowl'—the ducks and geese—most of whom are migratory and who only visit us in winter. You'll meet other swimmers and divers like pelicans and cormorants and darters. You'll meet spidery-footed jacanas or 'lily trotters' who can walk easily on floating vegetation. You'll meet bejewelled kingfishers, graceful terns and garbage-eating gulls. And you will also meet a few of the fierce clan of raptors—the birds of prey—who feast not only on the fish in the water, but more so on the water birds and their babies...

I have not included seabirds in this collection, so—apart from gulls—you won't meet any of those here.

You can watch water birds at nearly any water body—right through the year. The monsoon is a specially good time for resident water birds, because this is when most of them breed. Egrets put on their lacey finery; storks, herons, cormorants, spoonbills and ibises bring up their broods in teeming, noisy (and very smelly!) colonies. Almost immediately after the rains, the first of the migratory birds arrive—great skeins of waterfowl and waders—from the now inhospitable wastes of Central Asia and Eastern Europe.

Sadly, we are not really taking care of the habitats that water birds live in. These 'wetlands' as they are called, may be marshes and swamps, rivers and streams, estuaries, mudflats, lakes, ponds, village tanks and even roadside ditches! We are busy draining them and turning them into fields for agriculture, or plots for housing or industrial complexes. Apart from attracting birds, these wetlands are vital for the storage of rainwater and prevention of drought.

Also, we have poisoned and polluted most of these wetlands enormously. Most of our great and holy rivers are nothing but great stinking sewers, and the marshes have been turned into garbage dumps. Even that greatest water body of them all—the ocean—has been disgustingly sullied by our activities. This has played havoc with the population of water birds, not only in India but all over the world. When I see a blackwinged stilt hunt in the mud in the Jamuna in Delhi, I shudder. Just what kind of poison is that bird consuming and what effect will it have on its eggs and its young in future, I wonder.

While you can watch water birds at any decent water body, some places of course, are especially wonderful. There's the Keoladeo National Park at Bharatpur, as well as Chilka lake in Orissa, Pulicat lake in Tamil Nadu and Andhra Pradesh, Sambhar lake in Rajasthan, Harike in Punjab, to name just a few.

You will need a fairly powerful pair of binoculars (one with a power of 10 x 40 for example) to enjoy watching water birds, because they do tend to stay quite far away.

And when you return home in the evening, after a day out on the jheel or lake, tired and hungry, you will be filled with a strange sense of exultation and happiness, like a light glowing inside you. Your spirits will be high and you'll be murmuring or humming to yourself as happily as the fat ducks there back at the water. Water birds can have that kind of an effect on you.

Made for Mud and Water

M OST WATER BIRDS ARE SUPERBLY AND SPECIALLY equipped to live on, or near water and mud. Not only that, the various species are also so equipped that they do not interfere or compete with each others' lifestyle or diet, in a way that could prove harmful to each other. Here, we will take a brief look at just some of the specialised equipment they have developed for their very special way of life.

The feathers of ducks and geese are waterproof, thus enabling them to bob buoyantly on top of the waves, upend or dive in the water, without fear of their feathers becoming soggy, and putting them in danger of drowning. Actually, their feathers are made waterproof by the application of oil from a special gland near the base of the tail. Instead of oil, herons use 'powder down' which is a powder-like substance caused by the crumbling of certain special feathers just for this purpose. These feathers continuously grow and crumble, providing a supply of this powder which the bird then applies all over its body. Powder down makes the feathers waterproof and keeps eel slime off the plumage.

Darters and cormorants, however, don't have waterproofing equipment and their feathers actually absorb water like a sponge. This makes the birds heavier and thus, enables them to dive deeper (more than 100 feet) after fish. But after four or five dives, these birds have to spread out their wings in the sun to dry or else risk death by drowning because they get too heavy and can't keep afloat anymore.

The dabchick or little grebe can vary the level at which it floats in the water. If it is happy and confident, it fluffs up its plumage, trapping air in its feathers, and bobs high on top of the waves. If danger threatens, it squeezes out the air, and sinks deep, with its back barely breaking the surface of the water.

It is in the design of bills and feet that specialisation in water birds has really taken wing! Ducks and flamingos have bills designed to filter small living creatures from the water. Most of the waders have long, pointed sharp bills, designed to probe the mud. However, the bills of different species of waders are of different lengths, enabling them to probe the mud at different depths, where different delicious squishy things live. Thus, godwits have long Pinocchio-like bills enabling them to probe perhaps 10 centimetres into the mud, while plovers have relatively short bills enabling them to pick up creatures just beneath the surface. And between these two extremes lies the food supply for sandpipers and redshanks and others, whose bill-lengths also lie between these two extremes.

Pelicans have huge shopping-bag cum dip-net bills: indeed their bills really can hold more than their bellies can! Herons and egrets have sharp spear-like bills and kingfishers are armed with deadly daggers.

As for feet, well ducks and geese have their famous flipper feet which enable them to paddle briskly in the water, and help them to dive or dabble. It does mean however, that they waddle hilariously on land because the feet are set so far apart and are located right at the rear end of the birds. Jacanas have long spidery toes which helps them walk on floating vegetation; flamingos have legs and feet that are specially tough and can withstand being immersed in ferociously powerful salt water (brine) where the algae they relish, grows. The osprey, a bird of prey who lives on fish, has spikes on the soles of its feet to help it grip better the slippery fish it catches.

Journeys Across the Skies

WATCHING THE ARRIVAL OF A FLOCK OF MIGRATORY ducks, or a large squadron of cranes over a lake, at the beginning of winter, is an experience that is unforgettable and one that leaves you feeling very humble indeed. You look up at the speeding masses of ducks arrowing overhead, or the long ribbons of cranes, flying past in perfect formation, with dignity and grace, and you begin to wonder...

Where have they come from? How many thousand kilometres have they flown? How do they know where to go and how to find their way there? Don't they get lost? And why have they embarked upon these immensely long journeys in the first place? What dangers have they faced on the way? How did they know that it was time to fly? Where were they yesterday and when did they start their journey? When did they last eat? How far do they fly everyday and at what height and speed do they fly?

And even if we do know the answers to some of these questions, bird migration remains one of nature's most fantastic spectacles and enduring annual events.

Many of the species of waterfowl and waders you will meet in this book are migratory. They breed in the vast food-rich areas of Central Asia and Europe, some going right up to the Arctic circle for this purpose. As there is food and space aplenty, and the weather is good, and the hours of daylight numerous (maybe even 20 hours of sunlight in a day!), there is plenty to eat and lots of space and time in which to hunt. The chicks thrive in these ideal conditions. But once the freezing fingers of winter begin to clutch, everything changes. Water bodies become sheets of cold slippery ice. The ground turns rock-hard. Insect and plant life dies out and disappears. The days become short and gloomy. Now there is little left to eat, and just a few hours of daylight to find food. Icy storms whip across the frozen wastes. This is no place for birds any longer.

So, off they go, flying south, to lands where the sun is balmy and the water bodies rich with food. It is said that it is the reduction in the number of hours of daylight which gives the signal to the birds to be off, by triggering travel urges within their bodies. (I suppose it's something like when you know exactly when to go to the bathroom!)

But how do they find their way? We know that birds use the sun and stars to navigate by, as well as the earth's gravitational and magnetic forces. They also use landmarks—following mountain ranges, coastlines, rivers and so forth. But exactly how all these direction finding systems work together so flawlessly remains a mystery.

Some birds are born knowing exactly in which direction they have to fly. Others know it partially, and learn the exact route from their parents. The larger birds—like the geese and cranes—may fly by day, the smaller waders fly by night. They fly at altitudes ranging from 500 to 1,000 metres above sea level, though geese have been spotted flying right over the mighty Himalayas while taking shortcuts to India! They fly at speeds ranging from 50 to 100 kilometres per hour. Some birds fly enormous distances non-stop—while flying over oceans, for example. While birds like cranes and geese must regularly land to refuel while on the way, smaller birds like sandpipers stock up huge amounts of 'fuel' for the journey by eating till they are twice their normal weight! The fuel is stored in the form of little balls of fat in their bodies, and some of their body organs, including the brain, actually shrink to make room for the fuel supply!

Sadly, migratory waterfowl and waders are shot in the thousands while on their epic journeys. For long they have been considered good eating and 'sport'. In the old days, the slaughter of massive proportions used to take place all over the country. One of the most well-known places for this in India, was the Keoladeo Ghana at Bharatpur—once the shooting preserve of the Maharaja of Bharatpur. Thankfully, today it is a National Park where nothing of the kind is allowed.

In India, the main route for migratory waterfowl and waders lies through the river valleys of the Indus and the Brahmaputra at the western and eastern ends of the Himalayas. Our migratory water birds arrive from the wetlands of Central Asia, Siberia and Eastern Europe, some flying 8,000 kilometres each way. We know the exact places some of these birds come from thanks to ringing. The birds are caught in invisible mist nets and a small metal or plastic band is placed around their legs. Then they are released. The band has the name and address of the organisation doing the ringing—in India it was the Bombay Natural History Society. If the bird is later recovered—or caught again—the finder is requested to return the ring with information as to where and when the bird was found. Today, scientists are fixing tiny radio transmitters on migratory birds, in an attempt to exactly track their migratory routes with the help of satellites.

Our first migratory guests begin arriving by July or August. By October and November, the migration is in full flow, and the birds stream in through the river valleys and then spread out over the huge subcontinent. They may stop over at favourite spots while on their way, before finally arriving at the very same jheel or tank that they had come to the previous year. Here they will remain till about March or April, enjoying the pleasant weather. But as it gets warmer, a great restlessness seizes them once more. Ducks begin swift practice flights and the long-legged, long-billed waders begin another feeding frenzy, stocking up on fuel for the return journey.

And then one morning the jheel or tank that was so alive with birds is suddenly empty, and lies forlorn and mirror-still. And high above, swift squadrons fly past, heading north, intent on their journey home once again.

Of Paddling Princes and Paupers

GREAT CRESTED GREBES

THE SMALL LAKE WAS CALLED RATAN TALAO AND WAS located near Sambhar lake, India's largest saline lake, some 60-odd kilometres from Jaipur in Rajasthan. It should have been quiet and peaceful on that early Sunday morning except that all the parakeets in the district were holding a panchayat meeting in the huge banyan tree that overshadowed the lake. My attention however, was not on the parakeets' arguments; it was riveted on two slender aristocratic birds gliding over the waters of the talao, looking like a pair of princes every inch of the way. (Of course, one of them must have been a princess, but she looked like a prince, if you know what I mean.)

They were great crested grebes and this was the first time that I was seeing them. About the size of normal ducks, they had dark grey-brown, shawl-coloured backs and foreheads—which sloped stylishly upwards—and silky creamish sides. Short ear tufts on either side of their heads made them look a bit like characters from *Star Trek*. Their necks were long, slender and

GREBES
1. Great Crested Grebe, 2. Black-necked Grebe

straight, and their sloping foreheads made it seem as though they were looking down their noses at everyone. They had no tails to speak of, and they glided over the pond elegantly, keeping aloof from the quarrelling egrets and pond herons that were also present.

I also knew that they weren't looking their best here. That would be during their breeding season, between June and August, and I would have had to go to the high altitude lakes of Ladakh (at heights between 4,600 and 5,200 metres above sea level) to see them then. At that time, their blackish ear tufts become really prominent and they wear a stunning frill or ruff of russet and black feathers around the nape of the neck and throat. While courting, both partners first approach each other, their necks held stiffly straight, their ear tufts sticking out dashingly, their ruffs flared. Then both dive and surface with weeds in their beaks and then suddenly, sort of stand up in the water, breast to breast, and sway. No, they're not daring each other to combat, but declaring their love for one another. Both male and female are dressed alike.

During winter they lose their fine costume and migrate to lakes and talaos in northern and central India, flying down south as far as Maharashtra and north-eastern Andhra Pradesh. Frankly, there's nothing better to give a lake a bit of class than a pair of these elegant princes sailing serenely around, and it's a shame it is so difficult to see them when they're looking their glamorous best during the breeding season.

If great crested grebes are the princes of lakes and talaos, then little grebes or dabchicks must be the paupers! They're stumpy little water birds, with short pointed bills, and legs where their tails ought to be! Their rear ends are all fluffed up and raised, and if you stare at them too hard and too long, they'll do a neat headfirst somersault and disappear underwater. During the breeding season (April to October in northern India; December to February in the south), they are a rich dark brown on top, the sides of their neck, throat and head shining silkily, a lovely wine colour. Below, they're dusky white. Their bills look swollen and are yellowish green. When they're not breeding they turn drab brown.

Dabchicks are found on water bodies pretty much everywhere in the country—usually in pairs or small groups—and occasionally in larger number on the bigger jheels. Often, you become aware of their presence by their shrill alarm-clock-like trilling call, which is a sound most often heard around ponds and lakes during the rains.

Dabchicks have a number of endearing and funny customs. They build their nests, a pad of soggy, rotting vegetation, half in, and half out of the water along the edges of ponds and lakes, affixed to reed stems (so they don't float away!). You'd imagine their eggs and young would catch chills and maybe pneumonia in such a damp home, but apparently the heat generated by the rotting vegetation through the process of fermentation (like in a compost heap!) prevents the eggs and chicks from getting chilled. When the chicks hatch, they're first fed with feathers, which can't be very delicious, and which they will continue eating throughout their lives. It is thought that the feathers protect the birds' delicate stomach and intestines from being harmed by sharp fishbones and crab shells that they may subsequently eat. (Rather like gulping down wads of bread to help a nasty fishbone down, except in the reverse order!) Dabchick babies—about five or six is the usual family size—are able to swim within a day of hatching and are happy at first, to be towed along by their parents, latching on to them with their beaks. If danger threatens, the parent will dip its bum low into the water providing a gangway for the chicks, who will clamber on board and snuggle safely into the feathers on their parents' backs. Often, they go riding around like this, and are even fed while on piggyback!

Dabchicks eat small fish, tadpoles, crabs and aquatic insects. Often a pair will bring up two sets of young in succession; when this happens the father looks after the chicks that hatch first, once the mother begins incubating the eggs of the second lot. The birds prefer paddling to flying (and can hardly walk), though when forced to fly are fast, powerful flyers.

I've always enjoyed the company of dabchicks. I remember watching them at Badhkal lake near Delhi. There, on this huge dark blue ocean of a lake, made feisty by a stiff breeze and looking seriously deep, were these tiny endearing little things bobbing about confidently like cockle-shells in the Pacific, turned to gold by the rising sun. They seemed to be enjoying themselves thoroughly and every now and again would do their little headfirst leap and disappear underwater, leaving me to guess where they would pop up from again.

Watching Flying Boats at the Zoo

WHENEVER I GO TO THE ZOO IN DELHI (TO BIRDWATCH), I make sure that I'm at the pelicans' pond by around 10 o'clock so that I can watch the great white or rosy pelicans take-off. Usually, at this time the group of ten or twelve birds will be clustered in a pale pink huddle in the middle of the lake as though listening to cricket commentary on a very small transistor. Then one by one, they will break free and (presumably) the squadron leader will sail to one end of the lake. Here he will turn around and face the wind and begin to flap his big wings (revving engines so to speak!). Then he'll begin to taxi for take-off, paddling furiously with his webbed feet, wings thumping up and down. You watch with bated breath as he splashes towards the trees at the end of the lake, still not airborne, even as the second bird begins to follow him on the 'runway'. Then suddenly he is clear of the water and banks away from the trees, flying back over the lake again, his beautiful black-bordered white wings whooshing a steady beat, his immense bill making him appear to be smiling widely. His second-in-command follows suit, and soon most of the squadron is up and away. With their heads laid well back on their shoulders, and beak resting partly on the folded neck, they look immensely relaxed as they fly. If they are in the mood they may hitch themselves to the thermals (rising bubbles of warm air) as the vultures do and indulge in an hour's soaring, looking like tiny white crosses against a clear blue sky.

But all this, alas, is tinged with sadness. For there on the lake flap the remnants of the squadron—the pelicans that have had their flight feathers removed by the zoo authorities, and who are now flapping on the water in hopeless circles, baffled that they can't get airborne. I think that the zoo authorities do this to ensure that at least some pelicans will always remain at the pond, and that these birds will encourage the free-flying ones to come back after their flight, which is exactly what they do; soon they're circling low over the lake, and extending their feet forward, splash down, always looking as though they're a little bit out of control and coming down too fast. All of this makes it even more exciting to watch! With their broad wings and streamlined keels they have always reminded me of flying boats. While on their long migratory journeys, pelicans fly in the classic 'V' formation or in long echelons (chains) strung out across the sky, perfectly synchronising their wingbeats (like you do with your arms and legs while marching!). This method is said to enable them (and other birds that fly like this) to conserve energy while flying. The air currents caused by one bird's wingbeats helps to bouy up the bird immediately behind it. The leader, who gets no such help, switches position to the back when he gets tired.

PELICANS
1. Great white Pelicans, 2. Dalmatian Pelicans, 3. Spot-billed Pelicans

Great white, or rosy, pelicans have dazzling white plumage delicately tinged with pink, and their huge shopping-bag bills are yellow. They have pink-rimmed bright button eyes with a humourous twinkle in them, and wear absurd little crests that make them look even more comical. Rosy pelicans breed on the Rann of Kutch and spend the winter in jheels, lakes and lagoons, mainly in the northern part of the country.

The more common grey or spottedbilled pelican is also a resident species but breeds in south or south-east India between mid-September and April, and spreads throughout the country during the rest of the year. It is grey, or greyish-white all over, with a brown crest, and doesn't have black on the wings. Its beak has large black spots on its top half (mandible) and its elastic pouch is of a purplish bruise-like colour.

While the rosy pelican nests in colonies on the ground, the grey pelican does so on trees. Kolleru lake in Andhra Pradesh has been one favourite nesting colony for these birds. Both parents bring up the three or four young ones who in their early days, look exceedingly ugly, like rejects from Jurassic Park.

Actually, pelicans seem to be very military-minded (if funny looking) birds, because they do nearly everything—preening, foraging, resting—together. What one bird starts doing, the whole flock must do. And apart from watching them fly together, I love watching them fish together.

First they get into a wide horseshoe or crescent formation ('Form a crescent!' as the Romans would bark in *Asterix*) in the middle of the lake. Then, on a pre-arranged signal, they begin beating their wings on the water and swimming towards the shore, gradually closing the mouth of the horseshoe (like one closes a pair of pincers or pliers!), enclosing and trapping the hapless fish. Once the fish are jumping about in panic in the shallows, those huge shopping-bag cum dip-net bills are plunged and scoop left, right and centre! And yes, the pelican's bill can indeed hold more than its belly can! More than 11 litres or three gallons, two or three times as much as its stomach! The birds need about two kilograms of fish everyday.

Apart from being used as a fishing net, the loose, flappy skin (called the gular pouch) of the bill helps keep the birds cool. They flutter it like a wet fan when hot, and the resulting evaporation and breeze helps cool them down.

These smiling comical birds add charm to any lake or lagoon, but sadly some are threatened with extinction because their nesting areas are being destroyed by us. The poor spottedbilled pelican is in fact, regarded as being 'globally threatened.'

Sinking Sea Crows and Drowning Bald Ravens

SINKING SEA CROWS AND DROWNING BALD RAVENS? HAVE I gone nuts? What the heck are crows and ravens doing in a book on waterfowl and waders in the first place, let alone sinking and drowning ones?

Well, actually I'm talking about cormorants. You know, those glistening black, wet-looking birds you see near jheels and lakes and talaos and tanks, often perched on rocks or bare branches with their wings spread out as though they were being crucified. Or swimming strenuously in the water, weaving from side to side, and floating so low that only a slice of their backs and the tops of their heads are visible above water. And just when you think they're about to go under like a sinking kayak, they actually do, and that too, with a little headfirst leap. So have they indeed sprung leaks and sunk swiftly to the bottom, and will their bones eventually glimmer on the bed, like the skeleton of some ancient Lilliputian shipwreck?

CORMORANTS

Not a chance! If you take a peek at a cormorant underwater, you'd see it swimming swiftly (with its wings) in pursuit of some poor fleeing fish. Once the fish is caught by that long hook-tipped bill, the bird heads for the surface. Here it tosses the fish into headfirst position and swallows it. Then down it dives again, and again, till its tummy is full. But by now, believe it or not, the cormorant really is in danger of sinking and drowning to death! For its feathers, unlike the feathers of other water birds such as ducks, are not waterproof—in fact, they're more like a sponge and absorb water making the bird dangerously heavy—and sinkable! Also, cormorants don't have a preen gland like other water birds, which provides special oil (like Vaseline I guess) to make the feathers waterproof. So now, soggy and waterlogged, this goofy looking black bird just has to get out of the water fast. (Pneumonia is another danger!) It flaps its wings, paddles its webbed feet frantically and speeds over the water. At last it is airborne and flying swiftly and strongly, head thrust forward purposefully. It finds a suitable perch or rock and settles down, spreading its silky wings out to dry.

It has also been thought that this rather heraldic posture enables the cormorant to balance itself better (otherwise perhaps it would tip over backwards or fall flat on its face) and helps it to digest its food (which is always fish).

Cormorants like living in groups and even go fishing together like pelicans, and nest in huge, smelly colonies alongside egrets, herons, storks and other water birds. There are three kinds found in the country (out of around twenty-two in the world)—the little cormorant, the shag—also called the Indian cormorant—and the large cormorant—which again, is also known as the great cormorant.

The little cormorant looks somewhat like a jungle crow who has been doing too much bungee jumping—it looks a bit stretched out! It has a longish, stiff tail, and (unlike a jungle crow) a beak that is sharply hooked at the tip. It has a small white patch on its throat and the faintest hint of a crest. In north India it nests between July and February, in south India between November and February. The shag is larger and in the breeding season (between July and February depending on the area) wears fancy white feather tufts behind the eyes and white speckles on the head and neck, which some people felt made it look well, shaggy! The large cormorant is almost as large as a goose and in its breeding season (between September and February) has white cheeks and large white oval patches on its flanks which you can see clearly as it flies past. The bare skin under its beak (called the gular pouch) is a bright waxy yellow. It's quite difficult to tell apart these three musketeers in the non-breeding season because they lose all their feathery tufts and white markings, unless of course they arrange themselves in height order for inspection!

I've often felt that cormorants look like statues made out of bronze: their feathers have a metallic greenish tinge to them and look scalloped, like metal shingles on a roof. And then of course, there is the dramatic heraldic posture they adopt, with wings outspread, looking rather like goofy black angels on tombstones!

Cormorants build untidy twiggy nests and both parents look after the four of five young that hatch. Baby cormorants (who look ghastly in their early days) will grab their parents' bills and shake them vigorously until their parents throw-up (regurgitate is the word for it) semi-digested fish which is gobbled up quickly. Their colonies are noisy, smelly places, what with offal, droppings, rotting regurgitated fish and flies…Yuck!

But wait! The droppings (called guano) of certain cormorants nesting in the Peruvian islands of South America make excellent fertilizer and are worth a great deal of money. Also, in China and Japan, cormorants have long been trained to catch fish for fishermen. A string is tied around the bird's throat to prevent it from swallowing the catch which it obediently regurgitates for the fisherman. At the end of the trip it is of course, rewarded. The fisherman removes the string and stuffs fish into the bird's throat—and then reties the string around the throat above the fish to ensure that the bird swallows them instead of automatically spitting them out as it has been so expertly trained to do. Fishing with cormorants is however, going out of fashion these days.

Ah, but I still haven't explained about the sinking sea crow and drowning bald raven! It's simple really. The name, cormorant, has been corrupted from the Latin name *Corvus marinus* which means, you guessed it, sea crow. And the large cormorant's scientific name—*Phalacrocorax carbo*—you guessed it again, means bald raven on account of the white patches on the head and face which make it look bald. As for the sinking and drowning bits, well you know about that already.

Cormorants can be found all over the country and often can be seen flying swiftly in large 'V' formations, or strung out in great wavy black ribbons across the sky as they make their way to and from their feeding grounds. It was thought at first, that they reduced the amount of fish available for us (as though all the fish in the water belong to us anyway!) but it has been found that the fish they eat are usually not the ones we catch and sell.

Sleek Submarine Spearer

THE SLIM, SPINDLE-SHAPED BODY, AND SLEEK WINGS ARE jet black with moon-silver streaks. The javelin-like head and neck, velvety chocolate brown. The chin and throat, whitish. The deadly spear bill—a lance ready to fly. The tail—coal-black, stiff and fan-shaped.

It looks like a sleek strike aircraft belonging to the airforce of Jurassic Park. But it is of course, the darter, an ally of the cormorant, also known as the snake bird, and one of my all-time favourite water birds. (Actually, it looks rather like a heron from the top and a cormorant from the bottom and it behaves a bit like both!) Like the cormorant, it too floats very low in the water as it swims, weaving that long sinuous neck from side to side like a serpent— the only part of its body that is visible. And it too lacks waterproofing in its plumage and must necessarily spread out its wings to dry after every major fishing trip, or risk sinking.

And again, like the cormorant, this fighter-plane of a bird attacks not in the air but under water. It is a submarine striker. Unlike the cormorant who does a little headfirst leap before diving beneath, the darter slinks stealthily under water with not

DARTERS

a ripple. If it sights a fish—the only food that it consumes—it swims swiftly after it, wings half-open, paddling strongly with its webbed feet. When its target is within range, the deadly spear bill moves back and forth as the bird perfects its aim; then whoosh and wham! The bill streaks forward like an arrow from a crossbow, impaling the fish. The bird surfaces, jerks the fish loose with a shake of its head, tosses it and catches it headfirst before swallowing it. Sometimes the fish looks too large for the darter to swallow, but down it goes somehow!

Sometimes of course, the darter does not spot a fish as soon as it submerges. It dives down to the bed of the stream or the shallow jheel, and stalks the fish that are drifting carelessly past, in exactly the same sneaky, stealthy way that you may have seen herons and egrets do along the shallows and shoreline. Step by careful step... Then, whammo!

Darters nest in large colonies with the likes of cormorants, egrets and herons, though they seem to prefer reserving nesting trees for their own kind. In north India, they breed between July and December, in the south between November and February. Between three and six eggs are laid in the large platform-like twiggy nests.

On one of my trips to the Keoladeo National Park in Bharatpur (which is world famous for its colonies of nesting water birds as well as migratory ducks and waders), we were walking down the main road past the teeming, screaming colonies of cormorants, darters, herons, egrets and suchlike, wrinkling up our noses at the gross fishy stink. Then I spotted what looked like a forest of spears sticking out of the tops of some of the rather flat-topped acacia trees. I trained my binoculars on them and gasped. The 'spears' appeared to be the bills of darters all right, but the birds they were attached to were pure snow-white from head to toe, with pale powder-blue markings on the wings. They looked like a flock of slim, dangerous spear-wielding angels! But were they darters after all or something else? Then a regular, normal looking darter flew past the flock and all the angel darters frantically waved their spears at it, hoarsely squawking *chigi-chigi-chigi!* and grunting and croaking besides. The normal darter landed on a branch nearby, whereupon an angel darter nearby attacked it and thrust its spear-bill right into its mouth and down its throat, shaking it from side to side at the same time. The poor normal darter retched and threw up its fishy catch straight down the gullet of the greedy angel. By God, what a way to be stabbed and robbed!

The angel darters were of course, babies, some large enough to have left their nests, but not large enough to go fishing on their own. But boy, being a parent darter sure takes guts, and what a way to feed your kids! First you're in danger of being skewered by them, then they go and make you sick! And you may have to feed five or sick, sorry six of them!

For all their ferocity while feeding, baby darters are rather prone to suffering from mass panic attacks—huge bouts of fear and terror that they all get together rather in the manner of hay fever! If they are suddenly frightened—perhaps by an eagle swooping down or a human being approaching too close—they are liable to tumble pell-mell out of their nests, half-fainting with fright, their tummies running dreadfully, splashing down into the waters beneath where they immediately play dead. Once the danger has passed and they regain their composure, they claw their way up the trees, using beaks, wings and feet, to hoist themselves into their nests.

That same day I saw the baby darters, I watched a beautiful sleek adult darter preen itself while sitting on a tree stump. And I was amazed by the thoroughness with which it went about the task. I don't think it missed cleaning or tidying a single feather, no matter how tiny, in its entire plumage. Its spearbill and long supple neck ensured that it could inspect and tickle even the most difficult-to-reach parts of its body, and it looked as though it were tying up its neck into complicated knots! It took more than half an hour at the job and the message I got at the end of it, was loud and clear: When you do something, do it properly and thoroughly. More specifically, when you have a bath, *use* that soap and scrubbing brush and don't forget the back of your ears! Like all other birds, darters have to keep their plumage in tip-top condition in order to be able to fly and fish successfully.

You can see darters on water bodies all over the country— sometimes wheeling about in giant circles high in the sky just for the fun of it. And if you see a forest of spears sticking out of the tops of trees near jheels, irrigation tanks, talaos and streams, the chances are that they belong to a squadron of these sleek flying submarines, taking time off between their deadly dives.

Those Crotchety Old Fishermen

HERONS ALWAYS REMIND ME OF CROTCHETY OLD fishermen standing (or sitting) hunched at the water's edge doing nothing all day except ruining their postures. I get this terrible urge to yell, 'Stand straight!' whenever I see one, its head buried deep in its shoulders, glowering away. But of course, much before I can do that, the bird spots me and springs into the air with a harsh irritable *quaarnk*! It flaps heavily off, neck folded into a typical 'Z' shape, to seek a quiet corner where it can continue to fish (or doze) or brood over the ills of the world.

Actually, the grey heron which is the largest of the clan you will meet here and stands 75 centimetres (almost 2½ feet) tall, is quite handsomely dressed—as far as fishermen go. He is clad in a smart, pale silvery-grey suit. The neck and crown are white, and he sports a snazzy, thin black crest (called the 'occipital' crest because it starts from the 'occiput' part of the head which is the base of the rear part of the skull). He also wears elongated black streaked white feathers on the breast which look a bit like the badly frayed and tattered remains of a shawl or stole. His great dagger bill and long legs are bright orange-yellow during the breeding season, and otherwise, a yellowish, and greenish brown. His partner is similarly clad.

If you want to watch a grey heron fish, you'll have to sneak up on it very early in the morning or at dusk, because that's when

GREY HERONS
1. Immature 2. Adult

it's most active. Now, it might wade stealthily into the water, raising one foot with great care and then placing it down, its neck stretched out, peering into the murky depths with its gold and black eyes. Suddenly, it freezes...then zing! the dagger bill flashes forward and there's a poor fat frog or wriggling silver fish clamped firmly between the mandibles of the bill. The prey is 'straightened up', so that it can be swallowed headfirst. If the heron is hunting in tummy deep water, it cranes forward (like a badminton player about to serve), and then bellyflops into the water with an undignified splash as it lunges after its victim. This always makes me laugh because it reminds me of a maha-snob bada-sahib all suited-booted, falling flat on his face in a muddy puddle!

Grey herons are found all over India and live alongside jheels, rivers, marshes, tanks and such water bodies. In the northern part of the country they nest between July and October, in the south between November and March. Bharatpur in Rajasthan, and Vedathangal near Chennai are famous for their heronries.

Once, in the Keoladeo National Park in Bharatpur, I saw a group of seven or eight grey herons, all perched on the tops of some acacia trees, all facing the same direction, and looking as though they were waiting for a conference to begin. I didn't give the matter much thought, and only much later discovered what might have been going on there. Apparently, before they start nesting and breeding in right earnest, grey herons gather together near the area chosen as the heronry, usually a traditional site where many of the previous season's nests are still intact. For a while, they just stand around doing nothing. In fact, this area is called the 'standing ground', and the birds are regularly joined by more of their kind. Eventually, they manage to work themselves up into the right mood for nesting and parenting, and begin reclaiming old nests, or sites where new nests will be built. Herons like returning to their old homes, which they re-decorate and re-do. (Sometimes, these platform-like twiggy nests become so large and heavy that they topple over. Imagine if you kept adding a floor to your house or block of flats every year!) Then the male extends his neck horizontally and vertically, clatters his beak and honks, and shows off his silky black crest, all in a very formal and proper manner. The female, after a bit of fuss perhaps, then accepts him as her husband. Eventually, three or four oval sea-green eggs are laid and incubation proceeds for a little over three weeks. Both parents share all the chick rearing duties.

Somewhat slimmer and smaller than the grey heron, is the purple heron, or as one bird guide told a friend of mine, the 'pulpul' heron. If anything, the pulpul heron is even shyer and more secretive than the grey heron, and is dressed so that it can be virtually invisible amongst the tall grass and reeds at the water's edge. Its body is a slatey purple, which can sometimes look more grey, and sometimes like an aubergine, or eggplant depending on the brightness of the sunlight falling upon the bird. The face and long neck are a straw-brown with black stripes running down the front and back. The head and crest are also black. It also wears long droopy tassles on its breast, which are off-white with chestnut and black streaks, and which look like the leftovers of a shawl clawed by a bear. The undersides of the wings—seen when the bird unfolds them to take-off—are a beautiful rich date-brown or the colour of resin from a pine tree.

As purple herons prefer hunting in squishy marshes more than their other relatives, they have longer toes which help them to spread their weight over the floating vegetation. But this also makes it more difficult for them to perch on spindly branches— and it's funny to see them try to keep their balance when they land on one.

PURPLE HERONS

Purple herons too, are residents of India, and can be found, near water bodies. They too nest in colonies, but seem to prefer the company of their own kind. In north India, they breed between June and October, in the south, between November and March. They also build platform-like twiggy nests and both parents share all the duties.

As the eggs of herons are incubated as soon as they are laid, the young hatch out on different days, and are thus of different ages. This is because if the egg were not protected by the parent immediately on being laid, it would either bake in the hot sun, or be filched by crows. Anyway, this means that the last laid egg hatches last, and the chick that hatches, the baby of the family, usually gets terribly bullied by its bigger brothers and sisters. Also, it often gets very little to eat and may even starve. The parents don't interfere in the bullying—they simply feed the babies who make the biggest nuisance of themselves—the bullies! Herons are not the only birds who hand out this apparently harsh treatment to their youngest ones. Ah, are you a youngest child? Bet you're glad you weren't born a heron then!

Now I'm going to let you into a juicy secret about herons…You know, these crotchety old fishermen actually apply make-up! It's called powder down, and it comes from a type of feather that is never shed, but which grows continually and frays continually at the tip into this fine powder. Powder down patches occur in pairs at various bare places on the bird's body—on its breast, rump and flanks. Many other birds also have powder down patches on their bodies, but none have as well-developed ones as the herons. The powder down is water repellant and is used for removing oil, grease and eel slime from the heron's plumage. I guess if you're covered with eel slime, you'll have to do something about it! The herons apply the down with their bills and comb their plumage with (remember this!) the claw of their third toe, which is specially flattened and serrated, and well, comb-like, for the purpose. So, like many hip young men, herons too carry their combs around with them.

Finally, about that dreadful hunched posture...Actually it's all for the good. The kink in the heron's neck is caused by the unequal length of the neck bones or vertebrae. It enables the bird to shoot forward its bill like a harpoon, and also (by enabling the gullet to slide behind or before the vertebrae!) to help it swallow prey that may seem far too large. So who cares if you look like a morose, bad-tempered old fishermen, slouched over the water, if you can go and harpoon a whale and then swallow it whole! Well, almost—that was the one that got away, of course!

In Camouflage Colours

IT'S HAPPENED TO ME COUNTLESS TIMES AND EACH TIME I'm taken completely by surprise. There I am, stalking stealthily, heron-like, along the banks of a jheel or river, eyes peeled, camera at the ready, confident that no bird can escape my steely heron-sharp gaze. Then, just as I conclude that there are no birds in the area that I'm patrolling, there is a sudden harsh croak—*wako!*—and a dazzling flash of white. And there's the pond heron or paddy bird, winging irritably away to seek a quieter shore. Foiled again!

But really, it's not my fault that I failed to spot the wretched bird. For this dumpy little heron, standing about 46 centimetres or 1½ foot tall, is dressed in camouflage khaki grey-brown, its head, neck and breast cunningly streaked like sheaves of straw in the sun and it stands stock-still, its lemon-yellow eyes fixed on you. Only when you come too close does it unfurl those dazzling white wings, which can so startle you. Actually there may be several pond herons standing slouched at intervals along a short length of a river bank or jheel shore. They always remind me of cops doing sentry duty along a road where some pompous VIP is to pass. Even when they're perched on trees, pond herons simply merge into the foliage in an uncanny manner.

But why should a bird that is so well camouflaged have wings so dazzlingly white that they can startle you? Well, perhaps that's the very reason: if for example, the camouflage hasn't worked, and the bird is in danger of being attacked (say by a heron-eating crocodile!) the sudden unfurling of dazzling white wings may startle the hunter, and give the bird just enough time to get away.

During their breeding season, which in south India is between November and February, and in the rest of the country between May and September, these dour looking birds put on a very impressive maroon plumage which is made of long, decomposed feathers that may droop to below the tail. It's strange really, because while it does look as though the birds are dressed in tatters and rags, they also look exceedingly handsome at the same time! Perhaps our fashion designers can get ideas from the pond heron! And to top it all, the bird wears this hilarious long crest that lies flat along the back of its head and which stands up absurdly when it gets all excited.

Pond herons like skulking near almost any kind of water body—be it a jheel, river, flooded paddyfield, road-side ditch, marsh or village tank. They nest in small colonies preferably with their own kind, and while they like hunting alone, they don't mind each others' company while roosting at night. Three to five eggs are laid in a not very substantial twiggy nest, and both parents sit on the eggs and look after the young. Adolescent pond herons—or what you would call teenage pond herons—are similar if more spotty than their parents, and sport the most hilarious looking spiky punk hairstyles —what I call the porcupine punk cut!

The Hush-Hush Herons at Witch's Water

I CLIMBED TO THE TOP OF THE SMALL GRASSY KNOLL ON the Hindu Rao Ridge, Chops, my boxer (the dog I had then), tugging impatiently at his leash in every direction. Around me, the gnarled acacias crouched and whispered in the moth-coloured gloom of twilight. Just ahead lay the large eerie pond which I called Witch's Water. From a distance, it looked like a tempting, beautiful clear blue lake. But up close, you could see it was poisonously filthy with sewage and trash and plastic bags. And anyway, the Hindu Rao Ridge was no place to linger about in after sunset.

But then I stopped short and pulled up the dog. 'Hold it, Chops!' I whispered urgently, staring at the pond.

At the edge of the pond stood a hunched squat bird, casting a knife-sharp reflection in the still water. A heron, I knew by its shape and bill, looking as if it were cast in stone. Or bronze actually, because even in the gloom I could discern a metallic dark green tint to its blackish plumage. Instinctively I knew it was not the pond heron or paddy bird.

It could only be the little green heron, now known as just the little heron.

A rare bird in Delhi, I knew. But I had to be sure. The next evening we reached the spot a little earlier, and this time I had brought my binoculars. After a bit of anxious scanning I spotted the bird again, very near the place I had seen it the previous evening. And that too was true to character, for green herons are creatures of habit and like coming back to the same spot time and again.

This time, thanks to the binoculars, I got a better look at it. Slightly smaller than the pond heron, its back and wings were dark blackish green, the feathers beautifully etched and marked in ivory white. The breast and underparts were creamish white, heavily streaked. A ribbon-like black crest lay flat along the head.

A movement caught my eye. From the shadowy reeds another heron crept out stealthily to join the first bird. A pair! A pair! But then something disturbed them, for with a soft *K'yek*! they took off, one after the other, and flew low over the water to vanish in the tangled mass of reeds and rushes at the other end of the pond. I saw this pair of hush-hush herons several times again, but always in conditions of near-darkness, and always came away feeling that I hadn't seen them *properly*. But still, it was nice to know that such rare birds could be seen just a few kilometres from my house, though it worried me that they had to hunt in that poisonous looking pond for their food (mainly fish and frogs).

And then, a few years later, I went to Goa and met these secretive hush-hush birds in bright sunny holiday conditions. As usual, the bird I spotted behaved as though it were a secret agent in a spy movie. It was skulking along the base of some mangroves growing at the edge of a creek. Keeping under cover as much as possible, but occasionally being forced to step out into the sunlight.

'Come off it, relax, this is Goa!' I urged it silently, but no, it continued its cloak and dagger progress along the creek. Till suddenly, it froze and craned its neck forward and the bill flashed like a switchblade.

Small froggy for breakfast!

On a trip to the Keoladeo National Park in Bharatpur a few years back, I encountered yet another little green heron, perched on a snag abutting the jheel along the main road, quite unconcerned by the hordes of tourists passing by, just a few feet away. And somehow, I felt quite disappointed—half the fun of spotting the bird was lost. I certainly much preferred it when it behaved like a secret agent not wanting to be seen!

Little green herons are found all over the country, but never in large numbers. They skulk about the edges of streams, lakes, ponds, swamps, coastal backwaters and creeks, where there is plenty of cover for them to hide in. They prefer hunting at dusk, and may spend the whole day standing slouched on a stump, brooding. They nest usually between March and September and it is thought that they bring up two families, one after the other.

I haven't been back to Witch's Water for some years now and wonder if the hush-hush herons still lurk about in the reed beds. Perhaps, one of these evenings, when the full moon rises early and the bats have begun to flicker, I will go and take a look...

This Hunchback Remains Hidden

MOST HERONS LOOK LIKE HUNCHBACKS (AND NEED desperately to straighten up) but the one which has really wrecked its posture is the night heron. What makes matters worse is that this otherwise smart looking bird is rather heavily and stockily built, and even its bill is thick-bladed and short. And as though aware of its dreadful stance, it remains hidden all day, deep in dense bushes or trees usually located near water. You really have to seek it out...And often, you'll find it slouched on a perch much nearer than you thought, staring at you balefully out of unblinking ruby-red eyes.

Yes, it's a smart heron this one, dressed in what could easily pass off as a policeman's uniform. Dark, metallic blue-grey above, ashy-grey and white below, black crown with black crest with two antennae-like snow-white plumes sticking out of the rear. Shortish heavy black bill and of course those eyes, which look like drops of sunlit wine...Still looking at you...

And if it doesn't like what it sees, it will slink off its perch, and fly off on short rounded wings, uttering an irritated *wock*! as it goes, its head still buried in its shoulders, looking a bit like a flying fox.

Night herons are found all over the country, and true to their name prefer the hours of darkness to hunt and forage in (for fish, frogs and insect larvae). They're found near jheels, tanks, ponds and streams and also, creeks, lagoons, estuaries and backwaters. They nest in colonies, either with their own kind, or along with egrets and storks as does one colony I know of at the Delhi zoo. Here, they nest deep in the heart of a copse of acacia trees that are surrounded by water, and it's amazing how easily you can altogether miss seeing them. I'm always surprised by the number of nests I find—but that's after really scanning the trees thoroughly. Here, and in the rest of north India, they nest between June and September, in south India they do so between December and February. The nest is an untidy, rough and ready platform of twigs, which the female builds and the males brings the material for. Three or four eggs are laid, and both parents look after their young. Immature night herons are very different from their parents; they are khaki-brown, profusely speckled, splotched and streaked with dark brown and buff, and can look a lot like pond herons. I was baffled when I saw them for the first time, in the Keoladeo National Park. I knew they were not pond herons, and couldn't imagine them to be night herons. Then I saw some adult night herons in the same trees being harassed by these 'unknown' ones, and immediately guessed what they were.

The Story of Satin and Lace and Saffron Face (And Lanky Legs, of course)

MANY-MANY YEARS AGO, THERE LIVED A LARGE COLONY OF snow-white egrets on a tree-shrouded island in the middle of a large swampy lake.

The tallest of them all, was Lanky Legs, the large (or great) egret, who stood proud at 75 centimetres or 2½ feet tall, and who had a sharp black and yellow bill and blackish legs. Lanky Legs like the others of his kind (some of whom had black bills) kept largely to himself and tended to look down upon the smaller—and shorter—egrets. He hunted like the other big herons (the grey and purple) did, and during the breeding season put on a fountain of shimmery white plumes on his back. His partner dressed in the same way.

The other (smaller) egrets thought they were terrible snobs. Especially Satin, the median (or intermediate) egret, who couldn't get over the fact that he was just a few centimetres shorter than Lanky Legs, but otherwise almost just like him. Still, Satin liked boasting that during their breeding season, he and his partner grew beautiful lacy plumes both on their backs as well as their breasts, which made them look even more decorative than the large egrets.

GREAT EGRETS

'Not decorative!', she snapped 'Gorgeous, darling! Gorgeous!'
But of course, Lace, the little egret and the smallest of them all
was not impressed.

'Bah!' he snorted. 'Big deal! Look at us, little egrets! We wear
cascades of lace on our backs and breasts too, so what!' He
preened and twirled, and added significantly, '*And* we also have
this fabulous crest made up of these two satiny snow white
plumes that hang behind our heads. None of you guys have that!'

'And,' added his partner, joining in, 'have you seen our
beautiful boots darlings?' She dangled a slim, black, scaly leg
over the water. She was right. It looked as though she was
wearing yellow plastic (and rather cheap-looking) boots. 'You
know, they're very useful for fishing. When you dangle them
over the water, all the little fishes swim over to gape and admire
them. Then zing and wham! You got 'em! Now beat that!'

Of course the fish didn't come over to admire those yellow
boots, they were just inquisitive. (And have you seen a bird
wearing yellow plastic gumboots?)

'Oh, you poor poor vain creatures, but you are all dressed
only in lily white!'

They all turned to look at the speaker who had joined them.
It was Saffron, the cattle egret, strolling up in his usual mincing
manner, a prissy expression on his face, his yellow bill up in the
air. 'Look at us cattle egrets, will you. Our heads and backs turn
saffron during our breeding season. And saffron you know is a holy
colour. And don't forget, we keep the company of holy cows...'

'Not to mention, dumb buffaloes too!' muttered Satin darkly
But Saffron hadn't finished.

'And in the jungles we walk tall in the company of the elephant and rhino and wild buffalo, who kick up insects for us to feed on. We even inspect their ears and remove their ticks and fleas and leeches! Not even those stupid humans would dare to do that!'

Ah, but there was something else that those stupid humans did dare to do. Very silently, a group of men surrounded the island late that evening.

'Look at all those beautiful lacey plumes!' exulted the leader.

'Not plumes,' corrected his lieutenant irritatingly, 'Aigrettes!'

'Whatever!' snapped the leader. 'They're worth twice the price of gold! Just imagine, in a few months time the rich and beautiful women in Europe and America will be wearing those plumes in their hats...'

'Not plumes! Aigrettes!'

'Shut up! And princes and maharajas and royal highnesses will stud them with jewels and place them in their turbans!'

At first light the next morning, just as the egrets were beginning to bestir themselves, the men opened fire with horrible rusty muzzle-loaders. After the firing stopped, men with bamboo staves swarmed up the trees and began whacking the survivors dead.

'Leave the chicks!' commanded the leader. 'We are not baby-bird bashers!' And so the chicks were left to starve or be taken by eagles.

The men stripped the birds of their beautiful plumes (well aigrettes if you will) and flung their bodies away.

'Come on,' said their leader exultantly. 'I know of another egret colony not far away...'

A horrible story, wasn't that? But true enough. Till about the 1930s egrets all over the world were being massacred for their plumes, till they were in danger of becoming extinct. Then, after fierce agitation by bird lovers, the idiotic fashion industry was made to understand that it was barbaric to slaughter the birds so that silly rich women and maharajas could decorate their hats and turbans. And egrets, who were coming close to becoming extinct, began increasing their numbers slowly.

The cattle egret began travelling the world—to the Caribbean islands, North and South America, Australia—either on its own or with the help of people. It is now a firm companion of herdsmen and their livestock and has become pretty useful to both. The birds remove ticks and leeches from cattle, who might otherwise get ill. They snap up harmful crop-eating insects from the fields, and fertilise the ground with their droppings. And if there's a cobra or tiger around, they fly off together, thus warning the herdsmen.

But no, they needn't always be found in the company of cattle, or riding bareback on rhinos. On one of my trips to the Keoladeo (Bharatpur), from where cattle had been banished (and there are no rhinos), I came across a flock of more than a hundred cattle egrets, and this is what I wrote in my notes at the time:

'In the fishing grounds, there is tension in the air. A hundred egrets are poised tautly, all leaning slightly forward, and keeping absolutely still. Newcomers drift in like enormous snowflakes, making those already present, croak with annoyance. Occasionally a couple of birds fly at each other, croaking, and usually the intruder drifts away.

'At other times, the egrets start their fishing dance: hopping about in the water, wings flailing in a snowstorm of feathers, trying to panic the hapless fish and frogs into the shallows where they are speared. Apart from sporadic croaks, this monumental game of statues cum hopscotch is played in absolute silence.'

Many years later in Goa, I was happy to discover a collection of egrets-all-sorts in a paddyfield near the house. This, I thought, would be a good chance to photograph them all together. Needless to say, whenever I took the camera along, they'd all be gathered at the far end of the paddyfield, too far away to photograph. And whenever I didn't have the camera along, they'd be distressingly close, near the road, glaring at me out their hard, expressionless eyes. They would at times, step on each others' toes (and nerves), wherein indignant quarrels would break out, with flailing wings, lunging necks and stabbing beaks.

Egrets nest in colonies, with their own kind and other water birds, during the monsoons; between July and September in the north, and November and February in the south. They build rather untidy, flimsy looking twiggy nests and lay three to four eggs which take a little over three weeks to hatch. Both parents share all the household duties. Egret chicks, I'm afraid, like those of other herons, throw terrible tantrums at feeding time—yelling and screaming and grabbing at their parents' bills and shaking them like a dog shakes a rat, until they throw-up. Absolutely disgusting! These lovely angel-white birds can be found, usually near water, all over the country.

Candyfloss Bottoms and Ragamuffin Grumpusses

WHENEVER I SEE ONE, I HALF-CLOSE MY EYES, PUT MY imagination into gear and start to grin. And what do I see in my mind's eye? A stooping bald old politician, with a tiny round head and gigantic nose (slightly downcurved at the tip) wearing a short white nightgown-like garment (patterned in black) with two tufts of candyfloss tacked on either side of his bottom. He has long, leathery pink legs and his tiny protuberent black-button eyes make him look a bit of a fool. Ah, maybe I'm being a bit unkind, but boy, this bird would sure be a cartoonist's delight!

Of course, when you open your eyes and use your binoculars, you'll see the bird and not an old politician, and a rather beautiful bird at that. So I was being rather nasty, which was fun anyway! But standing (or rather stooping) at around 90 centimetres or 3½ ft tall, the painted stork is one of our most common and attractive long-legged wading birds. Its tiny bald head is orange-yellow (and its face has a foolish expression!), the huge sword-like bill is waxy-yellow (and so like an overgrown nose!), and its plumage is white, beautifully patterned or filigreed with black lace (imagine, a white nightgown with black lace!). The wing feathers too are a glossy green-black, and right near the tail are the famous tufts of rose-pink candyfloss. Both male and female are alike.

PAINTED STORK
1. Adult, 2. Juvenile

Painted storks are commonly found at jheels, creeks, rivers and tanks all over India. The poor birds are mute as they have no muscles in their voice box. So, to communicate they rattle their huge bills at each other and make moaning sounds. Their young manage to create quite a ruckus doing this, and rasp and wheeze too, when begging for food.

Hotshot birdwatchers don't usually pay much attention to painted storks because they're quite common and pose no problem to identify. But I've always found it difficult to ignore them (after all, how many hunched old politicians are there who wear candyfloss on their bottoms and who really are beautiful birds?!), and always shoot off far too much film when I encounter them. On one trip to the Keoladeo National Park, I swore that I would ignore them and save my film for more deserving and rare species...

...And what happened? Well, you see it was the nesting season of the storks—and other water birds—and there was hectic activity in the nesting colonies on either side of the main road that runs through the park. A great opportunity for photography! But then the skies began to darken and thunder rumbled and grumbled ominously. Oh great, I thought bitterly, now I wouldn't be able to take *any* pictures, not even of painted storks which I wasn't going to take but still... Sure enough, it began to rain and showered for about half an hour. But then the big granite thunderclouds massed themselves over the eastern horizon, and from the west, the late afternoon sun shone through, clear and sharp and gold as brandy. And there, gorgeously lit up against the background of an angry sky, was

Bharatpur's leading colony of nesting painted storks. I took out the camera...

The vivid green acacia trees were laden with nests. At one twiggy top-floor residence, a stork had just arrived and was exchanging greetings with his partner who was comfortably sitting in the nest (presumably on eggs, so maybe not so comfortably after all!). He leaned forward towards her, arched his neck stiffly and partly opened his beak, and I thought, 'Oh my god, he's going to be sick all over her and then there'll be an awful row!' But no, he wasn't sick, and his partner stood up stiffly and did the same thing to him without being sick either, to acknowledge his greeting. At the next-door nest, a stork was very tenderly nibbling at the neck and breast of his mate who seemed to be in a state of utter bliss. And everywhere, storks and other water birds were rushing busily to and fro, carrying nesting material or food.

The painted stork chicks that would eventually hatch— between two and five in each nest—would have coal-black faces and bills, and look as though they were dressed in cotton wool. As they grow, this white cotton wool gets dirtier and dirtier, until the birds begin to look quite filthy and frankly, like ragamuffins! When they are small, they are very sensitive to the sun, and their ever-caring parents will crouch over them with their glossy wings unfurled umbrella-like over them to give them shade. If danger threatens while the parents are away, the chicks will all immediately be sick and collapse as if dead in their nests. When they are about three-quarters grown, they will clamber out of their nests and stand around morosely, flapping their wings for excersise and practice, waiting for their parents to return from a fishing trip.

The adults fish individually in shallow water. They'll prowl through the water, neck bent down, bill open like a gigantic pair of tweezers, half-submerged. Occasionally, they'll freeze, half extend a leg and wiggle it to and fro while at the same time flicking open the wing on the same side. This panics any prey that may have been lying still, and it flees, only to be snapped up by the jumbo tweezers just waiting for it to move. When about six to eight fish have been caught, the stork flies back home where the chicks quickly scramble back into the nest, ravenously hungry. They wheeze and rasp and pump their necks and heads up and down and flap their wings frantically as if they're just about to collapse with hunger. But their parent will just ignore them and stand at the edge of the nest as if in deep thought. For as long as half an hour this terrible torture (for the chicks) continues. Then at last, the parent leans forward and vomits out the fish and a lot of slimy stuff on to the floor of the nest and the chicks go gobble-gobble-gobble quite disgustingly. It is thought that the chicks are made to wait so that their meal can be pre-digested by the parent into a form of fishy baby-food, before it is thrown-up for them.

Here in Delhi, a colony of painted storks arrives at the zoo to nest every year around August. The newspapers get even more excited about this than birdwatchers, and grandly announce the arrival of 'Siberian Cranes at the Delhi Zoo'! The birds nest here under the ramparts of the Purana Quila, and stay on till around March. Sometimes I can see them soaring high in the company of kites and vultures, even from my house. In the south, painted storks nest between November and March.

Escargots — Morning, Noon and Night!

YOU CAN ONLY GET THEM AT ONE OF THOSE POSH restaurants where everything is written in French and the waiters look like stuffed penguins and smile at you glassily, as if you were something that had crawled out of the gutter... Escargots, I mean. But if you look up snootily at your waiter and order 'Escargots a la bourguignonne, please!' (provided you can pronounce it in the Fhranch whay!), you'll have him grovelling at your feet, because he'll know he's dealing with someone who has very good taste: a real connoisseur. A gourmet.

So what are they, anyway? Hope your mouth's really watering now, because escargots are snails. You know those slimy slug-like things that ooze their way about the garden, eating leaves and leaving a trail of silvery sticky snot wherever they go? Well, when *we* eat them in expensive French restaurants, we call them escargots, because they probably taste better when they are called that...

The openbill stork however, eats them morning noon and night! Big juicy, *squishy* ones! It loves them so much that its bill has been specially shaped to enable it to remove the juicy creature without breaking the shell. The two halves of the stork's bill do not appear to close properly and you can easily see the slit between them. That's because the two halves—called the mandibles—are slightly arched and do not meet flush with one another. While eating snails, I mean escargots, the openbill stork holds the shell firmly with the upper half of its bill, and with the sharp tip of the lower half neatly cuts the muscle that joins the snail's body to the shell and scoops out the snotty delicacy. It can do this even when the snail is underwater, and in fact, will even wash the snail in water by shaking its bill vigorously from side to side before swallowing it. When we eat escargots, we make a huge fuss, taking them out of the shells and cooking them with wine and herbs and vegetables and then stuffing them back into their shells and popping them in the oven and so on. Incidentally, openbill storks also eat crabs and frogs, but then so do we...

This is one of our smallest storks, standing about 68 centimetres—2½ ft—high, and is dressed mainly in white with purplish or greenish-black wings, tail and back. During the non-breeding season, the white parts turn smoky grey making the bird look as though it needs a session in the washing machine with plenty of bleach. Seen from a distance, you can often mistake it for the white stork, but the slit in the bill—like the eye in a huge needle—is one sure way of knowing what it is.

Openbill storks are our most common species of stork, and live throughout the country, near inland water bodies. They prefer jheels and marshes to river banks and tidal mudflats. They nest in colonies some of which, like the ones at the Keoladeo National Park, can be quite enormous, with over a thousand pairs of birds. In the north, they breed between July and September, in the south between November and March. Between two and four eggs are laid in the circular twiggy nest, and both parents share all the household chores. Like baby painted storks, baby openbill storks also can't stand the heat and must be shielded from the sun by their parents' half-unfurled wings.

While they're not very pretty to look at, it can be great fun watching them fly. Or more correctly, watching them land. Way up in the heavens, they'll suddenly appear to stand up in the sky. Their wings will be pulled half in, neck and head held straight and high, their legs dangling wide apart. Of course you can't just stand up in the sky and remain there, and down down down hurtles the stork, at a frightening speed, wobbling dreadfully. It may bank steeply and even side-slip, a manouevre that can leave your heart in your mouth: the bird flips over onto its side and drops steeply downwards. In no time, it is at tree-top height braking hard with its wings and touching down lightly on a branch. And you're left staring, and wondering whether it has butterflies in its stomach (in addition to snails!).

PS: Did you enjoy your escargots a la bourguignonne?

The Stork with the Smiling Face

I NEVER PAID MUCH ATTENTION TO THE WHITE STORKS AT the Delhi zoo, because well, most of the time they just stood around (often on one red leg) doing nothing, wearing pleasant but vacant smiles on their faces. They looked more like decorative garden statuettes than birds. Standing at just over 100 centimetres or 3½ feet tall, they are white birds with black feathers covering their lower backs and wings. Their long, thick-bladed bills are red (as if they had applied lipstick) and their eyes are large and dark—especially as compared to the tiny button eyes of some other storks.

Then one morning as I passed by their island enclosure, I heard a strange clattering sound. I looked around in surprise. At the far end of the enclosure, at the edge of the water, a pair of white storks stood facing each other, almost breast to breast. Both had thrown their heads right back so that their heads and bills were almost resting along their backs (like my dog Wag does when I scratch his throat). The two halves (mandibles) of the bill were clattering together and producing the sound. Gradually the head was brought forward, in an arc-like movement, and then taken downwards until it was nearly touching the ground—as if the birds were now touching each others' feet! It seemed like a very elaborate and formal way of greeting your partner and courting, I thought. But if you had no voice with which to say, 'Will you marry me?', then I guess this was the best you could do.

But I doubted very much if the white storks at the zoo would follow up their courtship by nesting. You see, white storks are migratory birds that arrive in India from Europe—Germany for example—around September–October and stay on till March–April. The ones at the zoo probably had their flight feathers removed, so that they were forced to remain here all the year through.

The birds that do visit India in winter can be found stalking about sedately in marshy areas and ploughed fields, looking for frogs (which, it is said, can't resist their red legs!), crabs, mice and sometimes fish. They also love locusts and grasshoppers which makes them a great friend of the farmer. But they are shy and wary birds while in India, which is quite unlike what they are in the countries where they nest.

In many European countries—like Belgium and Germany, for example—white storks are so tame that they are almost regarded as domestic birds, like chickens! This is because, for centuries they have not been harassed or harmed by people, and are believed to bring good luck to those on whose rooftops they nest. They are actually encouraged to build their large twiggy platform-like nests on the chimney stacks of houses. People even fix platforms and large baskets on to their roofs in the hope that the storks will nest in them. They are revered in the Middle East too where they commonly nest on the minarets of old mosques. It is popularly believed that they migrate annually for the pilgrimmage to Mecca.

White stork pairs are famous for their faithfulness to each other, and for returning to the same nesting site year after year, where they raise and bring up their families. And this is probably how the legend started about storks bringing home human babies too. The female lays between three and five eggs, which are incubated for a month. The chicks are ready to leave home in between eight and ten weeks' time. Both parents share all the household duties.

The birds are strong but relaxed flyers, and have been clocked at flying over 75 kilometres per hour by the Royal Air Force.

Gross but Rare: The Adjutant

*I*F THE WHITE STORKS AT THE DELHI ZOO BORED ME BY standing around and doing nothing, the greater adjutant stork I met there one morning, had no such intention. The gross, hunched fellow, standing between 120 and 150 centimetres—4 to 5 feet— tall, had somehow got out of his enclosure, and now fixed me with his cold yellow-white eyes (the sort that makes your own eyes water if you look at them). Step by deliberate step, he paced his way towards me, like some ancient disreputable pirate, dressed in a silvery-grey greatcoat and unwashed white collar ruff. His small head was bald and orangish, with a patch on the top that looked like a ghastly scab. His scraggy neck was the same colour, and a horrible pinkish sausage-like appendage (called the gular pouch) dangled macabrely from his throat. His huge wedge-shaped yellowish bill, the size of my arm, began to look more and more fearsome as he drew inexorably closer. It really was a heavy and formidable weapon.

Of course, I wasn't scared of him—what rubbish—but I thought that it perhaps wouldn't be wise to let him practise his sword-play on me, which appeared to be his intention. I beat a tactical retreat.

Happily you are not likely to be chased by this menacing, curmudgeon of a bird—who is indeed so like a crusty, choleric old man. Unhappily however, you are less likely to even see one outside a zoo (I haven't), in the wild, because these old fogeys have become really scarce in the country. Now, they are common locally only in the Brahmaputra valley in Assam, and are rare visitors eleswhere.

So why did I include it here, if there's not much of a chance of anyone seeing one, except in a zoo perhaps? Well, because there are so many tales about this bird that are worth telling...

Of course, it's an easy bird to recognise. For a start, you can't miss that awful sausage-like appendage that dangles from its throat. Well, we don't even know what exactly it's meant for (except to make the bird look gross), apart from the fact that it is connected to the nasal passage and is not used to store food (or even snot!). That apart, this solid, stooping bird is clad in iron-grey, black and white, and has somewhat scaly looking grey legs. If it is young (and handsome or pretty!), its eyes will be pale blue, and oh, so cold...

Ah, and how did it get its name? Well, it appears that in the days gone by, colonial British soldiers who saw the bird thought that it reminded them of their adjutants, or adjutant-generals, who were usually the unpopular officers in charge of keeping the soldiers' personal records, and who would enter all minor indiscretions in their reports. Both, the birds and the officers, had the same stooping posture and measured military gait, and ill-tempered attitude.

Actually, the crusty old adjutant has fascinated people for hundreds of years. The Mughal emperor Babar, was once brought one and reported that it became very tame, and wrote that it once swallowed a shoe, nails and all, and made similar short work of a chicken. A popular belief that has existed amongst local people since Babar's days, is that if you split the head of an adjutant (illegal, illegal, illegal!) before death, you may remove from it the famous 'snake stone' (or 'Zahar-mohra') which is a powerful antidote against snake and other poisons. (It is not known whether it works on the venom of principals and paper-setters and examiners.)

In the wild, adjutant storks are found on marshes, pacing up and down in their deliberate, military way, stabbing now and then at fish, frogs, reptiles and crabs. They are great carrion-eaters too, and armed the way they are, have little to fear from vultures and jackals, and will stalk off with the best titbits from a carcass. (The birds are also found in Africa and you'll see them in any wildlife film depicting a lion or cheetah kill.) During the nineteenth century, they were found in large numbers in Calcutta too, keeping the streets clear of garbage and dead animals. And during the rebellion of 1857, they were also reported from the Ridge in Delhi (very near where I now live), where a lot of the most bitter fighting took place. Incidentally, their long white feathers have been used by people for decoration.

While the birds do breed in India—now only in Assam, though earlier in Orissa too—it is thought that most of the adjutants seen in India are monsoon visitors that breed in huge colonies in southern Burma. The breeding season lasts from September to January and the birds build colossal nests with large twigs on the tops of trees.

Clumsy and ungainly on the ground, the birds are magnificent fliers with a wingspan the length of 'two men', as one observer put it. I've never seen them fly and know that the ones at the Delhi zoo will never do so, because their flight feathers have been removed.

They have a smaller cousin, called the lesser adjutant, who is more black than grey and has a slimmer bill and no dangling sausage. On the top of its head it has what has been described as a few 'elephant hairs', which makes it look quite hilarious. It is a resident bird, with habits similar to other storks. Like its cousin, it too is a globally threatened species. So far, I haven't been chased by one though.

The Thrust of the Black Sword

YOU CAN GET PRETTY HUNGRY AFTER A DAY'S BIRDING IN a place like the Keoladeo National Park in Bharatpur, and my thoughts were drifting towards the sizzling hot pakoras and tea we would have when we got back to the Forest Resthouse. At the moment however, I was enjoying watching a large flock of murmuring ducks-all-sorts on the waters of the marsh. Casually, I swung my binoculars around and suddenly stopped.

A tall, lanky black and white bird had sprung into view: it must have been around 135 centimetres or 4½ feet tall, and had a glossy black head and neck, not to mention a formidable black bill. It was stalking haughtily about in the shallows on spindly pinkish-red legs. I knew at once that it was the blacknecked stork—our biggest stork—and one that has become quite rare in recent years. But what it did next put my mind right off hot pakoras. It lunged and stabbed at something black floating in the water again and again, while stepping closer to the object, which now had begun flailing desperately... It was, I saw to my horror, a poor—and very silly—coot (see page 123) that had foolishly floated within range of that thrusting black swordbill. Now, there was raw red meat being pulled off the poor bird, which I hoped

was dead. The stork literally took apart—disembowelled—the coot, gobbling it down in great greedy gulps. Coots of course, are not the only things that these storks skewer and eat. Actually, they go in more for fish, reptiles, frogs, crabs and small animals.

These striking birds stalk about marshes, jheels, river banks, and occasionally, the coast, throughout the country. They're more commonly found in the northern parts of the country than in the south. Actually, they are becoming increasingly scarce everywhere.

I used to observe a pair regularly for several years at the Sultanpur jheel near Delhi. I

BLACKNECKED STORK

knew they nested somewhere nearby, because every year they would arrive with a gangly youngster (and once, with two of them) in tow. The youngsters were more brownish than black, and their white portions too, were dusky. They nest usually between September and December, building enormous edifices out of large twigs, 20 to 25 metres up on large trees. Three to four eggs are laid and both parents look after the chicks, and feed them by vomiting all over the dining table—which of course is the floor of the nest. (Imagine if your parents fed you that way!) Blacknecked storks like keeping to themselves, and usually maintain a healthy distance even between each other.

When they fly, they remind me of beautiful small gliders: their huge wings are pure shell-white with a black band through each wing, and they love soaring in huge circles high up in the heavens.

The Delhi Zoo has several blacknecked storks, which probably have had their flight feathers removed. When you get close to them (but out of range of that swordbill!) you can see that their glossy black plumage is tinted with dark greeny-blue and purple. The female's eye is yellow; the male's is brown. Often the birds squat on their shanks which makes them look as though they are kneeling down, except that their knees are located at the back of their legs and not in front!

Ibis in Crisis

AS THE BOAT DRIFTED CLOSER, I COULD SEE THAT THE
nesting colony of water birds we were approaching in the
Keoladeo National Park (Bharatpur) consisted chiefly of white
ibises—now renamed blackheaded ibises. They were birds
which always make me grin wickedly because they seemed to
be such complete buffoons. Hopeless cases, actually. First of all,
with their hunched doubled-over posture (which would beat the
herons hands down!) and leathery black heads and necks, and
large downcurved bills, they appeared so craven and submissive
in attitude that you felt that even a dove could bully them around.
Certainly, they were not at all regal or commanding or worthy
of respect. Secondly, they seemed so hopeless and clumsy in
everything they did—be it trying to feed their chicks or even just
landing on a branch without overbalancing. Yes, the ibis
appeared to make a crisis out of everything it did!

The ibises festooning the trees in this colony were nearly all juveniles, with spanking white bodies and coal-black heads, necks and bills. Their parents were much the same except that their heads were leathery and unfeathered and they had these deep scarlet streaks under the wings (armpits actually!) which made them look as though they had been slashed by a knife. While nearly all the youngsters had clambered out of their platform-like stick nests, they were still all demanding to be fed by their parents like helpless little babies.

I called them buffoons, didn't I? Well, if I had been living in ancient Egypt and called them that, I would have probably been boiled in oil! Ancient Egyptians worshipped the ibis as the god Thoth, whose duty it was to write the story of each and every human being in the world. I shudder to think what he might have written about me, (in hieroglyphics) after reading this! In fact, the bird has also been called the sacred ibis because of this.

Actually, ibises do deserve respect—they come down in history a long way, and appeared on earth some 60 million years ago—many times the length of time we humans have been around (and now think that we own the earth and everything in, on, and under it).

The blackheaded ibis is a fairly common marsh bird in India and can often be found near jheels, rivers, marshes, flooded fields, salt-water lagoons, and tidal mudflats. It likes the company of other long-legged waders like storks and egrets. It will squelch through the mire, with a somewhat chicken-like gait, its head buried up to the eyes in the mud, bill slightly open to pick up fresh (if muddy) delicacies such as frogs, small fish, tadpoles, juicy worms and insects.

IBIS
1. Glossy Ibis, 2. Blackheaded White Ibis

In north India, the birds nest between June and October, and in the south, between November and March. Two to four eggs are laid and both parents look after the brats. Unlike storks, ibis parents do not vomit baby-food all over the nest floor, but let the chicks take it straight out of their gullets. It may be more hygienic, but certainly seems more dangerous and the ibis parents appear to get extremely flustered during feeding time! (Well, if the darters can do it why not ibises?)

There is a colony of free-flying ibises at the Delhi zoo too, and I've often seen them hustling and bustling about, always looking slightly panic-stricken as though late for some vital appointment.

When they fly, ibises beat their wings rapidly, then glide for a bit, and then begin flapping again. I always get the feeling that they've suddenly forgotten that they have to flap their wings, and then start flapping again as a last ditch attempt at staying aloft!

The small group of black creatures flapping towards me, over the distant trees shrouding Sultanpur jheel appeared somewhat sinister. They looked like huge, slow-flying bats. Bats in black silk, with flashing white shoulder patches (or epaulettes) and orange-red skull caps. Bats that you might see leaving Dracula's castle at dusk. I trained my binoculars on them, a little puzzled. No, they were not monstrous Dracula bats, but birds. A flock of black ibises. As I watched, they circled a tree and settled down untidily on it. Quietly, I began to move towards them for a better look.

From closer up, I could see that they were smaller than blackheaded ibises, glossy black, with that white shoulder patch and slender downcurved bill. The orange skull cap on the bare black head looked like a crop of pimples or warts, and was not something I'd like to have on the top of my head!

Black ibises too are resident birds, found mostly all over the country. They prefer drier ground—near water bodies, though—and here, in groups of eight or ten, they pick up lizards, small snakes, scorpions, frogs, crabs and small fish (from shallow water bodies). They like their privacy and will set up home alone and apart from other birds, often taking over the empty nests of kites or vultures. Two to four eggs are laid and both parents incubate them.

Some shells have it: the iridiscent rainbow shimmer that you often see on a soap bubble. But here is a bird that has it too: well, something quite like it anyway. For the glossy ibis is a rich dark chestnut-brown bird with a metallic greeny-purplish sheen to its plumage which always makes me think it is made out of mother-of-pearl. Actually, it's just because the light is reflected off its feathers in much the same way it is broken up and reflected off a soap bubble or shell.

The smallest of our ibises, this one is both a resident bird as well as a migrant. Some birds stay in India all the year through and breed here, while others spend only the winter months here. They can be found almost all over the country, often tummy-deep in swamps and marshes, in groups of up to fifty birds. Happily, they are not very shy and may allow you to approach fairly close so that you can admire their shimmering oil-drop colours properly. While feeding in a paddyfield, they may look from a distance, like village women bending over while working in the fields. Glossy ibises eat frogs, worms, tadpoles, crabs and stuff like that. They breed in colonies with other water birds between May and July. Two or three eggs are laid and both parents do the incubating.

Funkypunky Spoonfeeders

MOST BIRDS SPOONFEED THEIR YOUNG, BUT THE spoonbill seems to go one up on that: it spoonfeeds its chicks by actually using a long-handled spoon! Because that's what its bill looks like—a long soup ladle actually and a nicely coloured black-and-yellow one at that. Actually, the bill is more useful for catching food than it is for feeding the young, but we'll come to that a little later.

This 60 centimetre—2 feet—tall, elegant, snow-white marsh bird has long black legs, and wears a yellow-orange scarf on its throat. The famous bill is about 20 centimetres long, and flattened and circular at the tip. During the breeding season the bird's breast is tinged with pale yellow and on the top of its head it wears a hilarious flopsy-mopsy crest that stands up and collapses in the most hysterical way imaginable. A baby spoonbill being ticked off by its parent would have a hard time

SPOONBILL

controlling its giggles. Because when the bird is angry, the crest stands up mohawk-style, and then, when tempers cool, it flops down untidily all over the bird's face like a muppet's mop. I can happily watch this happen all day and can't help thinking that spoonbill chicks really do have funkypunky parents.

The soup-ladle bill is used to catch small fish, tadpoles, crabs, shrimps, and suchlike stuff, using a specialised technique. A group of spoonbills will stand tummy-deep in water, apparently daydreaming. Suddenly, they'll all wake up together and wade manfully forwards, their bills half underwater, and sweeping from side to side in a semi-circular movement. The lower part (mandible) of the bill rakes up the mud at the bottom, and any creature that flees, is quickly snapped up. Actually, spoonbill hunting always reminds me of people using metal or mine detectors a little too recklessly.

Spoonbills are both resident as well as migratory, and can be found in the plains, near marshes, jheels and rivers through much of the country. They are absent in parts of the Northwest and Northeast as well as Central and East India. They nest in trees, in colonies along with other marsh birds, but often prefer having their own kind as neighbours. In the north, they breed between July and October, in the south between November and January. Three or four eggs are laid and both funkypunky parents look after the brood. Baby spoonbills only develop their soup-ladle bills when they are ready to fly.

The birds fly gracefully in long wavy ribbons or in 'V' formation, their wings shining a lovely pearl white as the sunlight filters through them. Often they cruise very high up in the heavens, like cloud-white lace against the blue vastness of the sky.

The Tutu Battalion's Corps De Ballet

The jeep cantered over the vast grey lake bed—a crazy paving mosaic of baked clay—throwing up dust as fine as talcum powder. Some distance away, we could see the lake bed darken, and the driver, spotting this too, slowed down: it could mean soft ground. Far, far ahead, near the horizon, sprawled the lake itself, glimmering blue-grey in the morning light, and merging with the sky. Or was it just a mirage?

Suddenly the jeep lurched sickeningly and began to sink. 'Out, out, out!' commanded the driver urgently, engaging reverse and revving the engine into an unholy howl. 'If the jeep bogs down here, it'll remain here!'

We leapt out and watched the jeep extract itself, throwing up huge clods of dark, evil-smelling mud from under its wheels.

The ground seemed firm enough, but there was a sinister sponginess to it too. This was the bed of Sambhar Lake in Rajasthan, our largest inland salt water—or saline lake, and supposedly, a winter haven for flamingos which is what we had driven all the way from Delhi to see. But where were they? Forget flamingos, there wasn't a single bird to be seen in this windswept briny wilderness. Disappointed, I looked at the ground. My eyes widened... There was bird dung scattered everywhere, interspersed with daisy-chains of bird footprints. And also, pale pink down caught in the clefts and cracks of the clay, tiny feathers being tugged every which way by the wind. Feathers that could belong to only one species: flamingos! They had been here!

And they were still here! For there, right on the very rim of the world, was the largest gathering of flamingos I had ever seen. Between twenty thousand and thirty thousand birds surely; tiny delicate wire-fine silhouettes against the edge of the earth. Parts of the huge concourse would suddenly drift across the sky and shimmer like someone rippling a giant pale-pink chiffon scarf.

'At last!' I muttered. 'The Tutu Battalion of Brigadier-Generals!'

Ah, let me explain that. First of all, you will agree that flamingos look like ballerinas. They wear short white, or pale pink, ballet skirts—which are called tutus. They have long slim ballerina-like legs and long slender necks and that typical proud ballerina stance. But they also march stiffly in great battalions—goose stepping almost! And their hooked 'noses'—well bills really—give them the profiles of rather haughty haw-haw

Brigadier-Generals. Just imagine—an entire battalion of Brigadier-General ballerinas! Of course, I've let my imagination take flight and am being extremely rude, or rather, politically incorrect, which is what they call rude these days. But some things about flamingos are even more bizarre and unique than I could imagine. But first, to the basics:

There are two kinds of flamingos found in India (out of six in the world); the 140 centimetre—or 4½ feet—tall greater flamingo, which is pinkish-white, with dramatic scarlet and black wings, and that typically bent pink bill, and long pink legs. The lesser flamingo, standing between 90 and 105 centimetres— or 3 to 3½ feet—tall, is not as graceful perhaps, but is more strikingly coloured. It has a deeper rose pink plumage, and a dark, almost black bill which is decorated with a tuft of crimson feathers around its base. It too has vivid pink legs. Both have webbed feet which enable them to spread their weight over soft glutinous mud without sinking. And thanks to their tough scaly legs, both can tolerate ferociously salty and caustic water which would simply burn the skin off the legs of other birds—and ourselves. And now, to some of their more unique, special features:

By far, the most unique part of the flamingo is its strange

GREATER FLAMINGO

boomerang shaped bill. Though the bills of both—the lesser and the greater flamingo—look similar, they are different in the details of their design. This enables the two species to eat different things while feeding together in the same place, and thus, not to compete with each other. Both species feed by inserting their bills upside down in brine and mud. Both have filteration equipment, in the form of hairs (or lamillae, which is the technical name) lining the inside of the bills. Both of them use their tongue like a piston to suck in, and expel, water. Water, rich with food matter is sucked in, the foodstuff is filtered out and directed towards the gullet, and the water squirted out again. The tongue in fact, shoots back and forth in a groove in the lower half of the bill at a phenomenal rate—twenty times a second they say! But while the lamillae and bill design of the greater flamingo are suitable for retaining small animal matter like insect larvae, tiny fish and shrimps and so on, those of the lesser flamingo are much finer and hold back microscopic blue-green algae and plant matter. In fact, the bill design doesn't allow larger stuff to enter at all. While the greater flamingo probes the mud at the bottom, maybe one metre deep, the lesser flamingo 'floats' its upside down bill (which has a deep, boat-like keel!) just inches under the surface of the water and sucks up the algae-rich soup. Thus, both species can feed in the same lake and not compete with each other for food. Naturally, the lesser flamingo prefers the more fiercely briny lakes, because it is here that the blue-green algae really blooms in profusion. Incidentally, this algae has a pink pigment which gives the flamingos their beautiful pink tinge. (In some zoos abroad, flamingos are fed concentrated doses of this so that they may appear more pink and attractive to us.) Also, this algae is extremely nutritious—it is none other than the spirulina algae that is being touted as the mother of all health foods by doctors and health-food freaks. We've only recently discovered this; the flamingos have known it for about 50 million years!

Flamingos flock to four main areas in India. About half a million nest on the Great Rann of Kutch in Gujarat. Other places where they can normally be seen in large numbers are Sambhar Lake in Rajasthan, Point Calimere in Tamil Nadu, and Chilka Lake in Orissa. But they are great wanderers and may be seen in smaller flocks in briny and algae-rich waters all over the country. I've even seen them on the Jamuna in Delhi, which is really just a filthy sewer and wondered if they came here to give themselves five-star food poisoning!

These military-looking ballerinas breed in the Rann of Kutch, in huge 'flamingo cities' that may contain half a million birds. The nest is nothing but a volcano-shaped mound of mud, about a metre high, in which one (and very rarely two) egg is laid. Both parents incubate for about 28 days. They often pick quarrels with their neighbours while doing so—as you would be likely to do if you're jammed cheek by jowl with half a million others! The parent talks to its chick as it hatches so that it learns to recognise its voice. The spunky baby is clad in a silky grey down suit and is high-spirited from the start. It is fed on a rich extract of algae-soup, as red and pure as blood itself. In about four or five days, its legs become strong enough for it to go trundling about, tiny wings outspread for balance. When around 10 or 12 days old, all the chicks in a neighbourhood are herded into day-night care centres or creches by a few adults, so that their parents can take time off. Sometimes, these flocks of youngsters move around in huge gangs, trampling and gobbling whatever comes in their path, and may even become a danger to adults still on their nests. Gangs of juvenile lesser flamingos however, usually move away from the main colony to islands or separate areas, and remain here by themselves till the time they are able to fly. They'll be over two months old when they do that.

Flamingos are terribly sensitive nesters and the slightest disturbance may make an entire colony abandon plans for nesting that season. An aircraft flying too low, or, as happens often in Africa, an adjutant stork pacing the lake's edge may be enough. They all have a collective nervous breakdown. They are preyed upon by animals of all kinds, as well as birds of prey, but hey, if there's half a million of you around, the chances of your surviving an attack must be pretty good. But no! They all— up and off. If they do survive up to adulthood, flamingos may live for over twenty years.

Ah, and now for the corps de ballet! That is performed of course, as a nuptial display, and the lesser and greater flamingos have their own separate performances.

Greater flamingos first gather near their nesting grounds in loose flocks. Then they all stand to attention—straight and upright, necks extended to the maximum, as if the National Anthem was being played. Now comes the 'eyes right! eyes left!' display, as they wag their heads from side to side. The birds look up at the sky and then very smartly, open and shut their wings. This display, apparently is called the 'wing salute'. (I told you they were military-minded birds!) The birds then preen and bow, again opening their winds so that the brilliant scarlet and black colours are displayed. After this, a group of birds may (though not very often) charge forward with the head and neck held like a shepherd's crock, calling and gabbling. This is called 'hooking'.

Lesser flamingos perform their displays in areas reserved just for this purpose, and which may be far away from their breeding grounds. For them, the wing salute, and bow, and hooking, are not all that important. Their 'piece de resistance' is different. A dozen or so birds will pack closely together so that the breast of one bird rests on the back of the bird in front of it, and the group will charge forward together through the colony. More and more birds join them as they career through the crowd, like I suppose, a huge multi-pink-legged corps de ballet playing chain-cook! They too may wag their heads from side to side and twist their necks into complicated knots.

These displays go on for months before the breeding season, which is between June and February for the lesser flamingo, and September to April for the greater. Whether the birds actually breed after doing their ballet depends on a whole lot of other factors, like the availability and suitability of the nesting sites, and of especially, their own peace of mind.

While flying, flamingos honk like geese, while feeding together they babble. It is a slightly menacing sound, this babbling, a sort of discontented muttering and mumbling—as though they're not very happy at being labelled Brigadier-General ballerinas!

Of course, when they fly, with necks and legs stretched out to the utmost, scarlet and black wings flashing, they look more like an avian corps de ballet, dreamt up by someone who writes nonsense rhymes about birds...

Trumpets in the Sky

Y OU COULD HEAR THEM EVEN ABOVE THE SHRILL CLAMOUR of hundreds of pied mynas settling down to roost for the night. A clear, uplifting hoarse yet musical bugling: *Krrooaah! kroaah!* As though big brass trumpets were being played in the sky. If you looked hard enough—towards the peach-gold west where the sun had just gone down—you could spot them: long wavy chains or echelons of large-winged birds flying steadily towards you. The cranes were coming in for the night, here at Sultanpur jheel (near Delhi) after having fed all day in nearby fields of wheat, pulses and groundnut. Here, they would be safe as Sultanpur is a National Park.

Now, it was wise to keep our heads down. If they spotted you and became suspicious, they would bank away and return only after dark. In any case, they would circle the lake two or three times, before lowering their legs, furling their wings and touching down in the shallow water or mud with an elegant hop, skip and jump. The great echelons would keep arriving till well after 9 o'clock and the birds would bicker and argue all night. There could be as many as six hundred of them, on and around the lake.

CRANES
1. Demoiselle Crane, 2. Sarus

You had to be back at the lakeside well before dawn, shivering in the winter chill, if you wanted to watch them take-off. As the cranes awoke and stretched and began calling, the lake began resembling a busy international air terminal. In the mauve pre-dawn gloom, you could make out long lines of birds preparing for take-off in different directions, like planes queuing up on various runways. One by one they followed each other into the sky, with lumbering effort, but becoming immensely bouyant and graceful as they gained height, with steady whooshing wingbeats. Within half an hour, the clamorous lake would be silent once again, except for the harsh laugh of a coot or moorhen.

We always made it a point to 'cranewatch' at Sultanpur, because it somehow always bouyed up our spirits for the whole day. These were common and demoisele cranes, both migratory species that had flown down from Central Asia and Siberia. The common crane is a tall (around 120 centimetres or 4 feet) grey bird with a black head and foreneck and reddish crown. It has a broad white stripe running down from behind the eyes along the sides of the neck, and flouncy black feathers falling over its bottom. The demoiselle crane, also grey, is smaller at around 100 centimetres or 3½ feet tall, flouncier and more stocky, and has a short black bill. It wears fancy white tassles behind ruby coloured eyes and a tattered black shawl at its breast.

Both these species migrate to India in the thousands, arriving by around September-October and staying on till March-April. They frequent large jheels, rivers and sandbanks, and are wholesale crop raiders. And so, are always exceedingly alert.

But they are wise to be wary, because they are shot and trapped in large numbers while on their long (maybe 5,000 to 6,000 kilometres) migratory flights. Crane hunters in the Kurram valley in Pakistan's North-West Frontier Province, through which the birds fly, use cords which are 30 metres long, with lead weights attached to the ends, to snare them. These 'soiias', as they are called, are expertly flung at the low flying cranes, entangling their legs and bringing them crashing down. The cranes are lured down (from as high as 2 kilometres up) by using tame decoy cranes on the ground. The idea is to catch the birds alive, but ultimately most end up in the market as food.

The reason why cranes can bugle and trumpet so hauntingly is because their windpipes are actually designed like trumpets, and have all their coils and wiggles! On a still day, their clarion calls can be heard from as far as 4 or 5 kilometres away.

The most famous crane to migrate to India, is of course, the beautiful Siberian or great white crane. Its story however, is a sad one, though some people still hope it might have a happy ending.

Siberian cranes, or 'sibeys' as they are popularly called, are tall (around 120–140 centimetres or about 4 to 4½ feet), elegant snow-white cranes, with black wing-tips and red faces. Always rare, these graceful birds would arrive at the Keoladeo National Park in Bharatpur every winter, where they knew they could feast on their favourite tubers that grew in the shallow waters of the jheels. In 1964–65, some two hundred birds arrived but ever since, the numbers have been steadily falling. Between 1969 and 1976, the numbers ranged between sixty and seventy birds between 1979 and 1988, between thirty and forty birds. By mid-January 1991, only ten birds arrived, and the figure was down to a dismal zero in the winter of 1992–93. However, in the following years, two or three birds did turn up every winter, though how long they will continue to do so—and whether their numbers will increase—is anyone's guess.

Apart from the slaughter they are subjected to while on their flights, another reason that is given for their decline is the reduction in the availability of their favourite tubers in Bharatpur.

To make their journeys safer, scientists have been trying to track the exact route the birds take while on their journeys. They sought to do this by fixing small satellite transmitters on the birds, but so far haven't been successful. They were unable to fit the transmitters on the wild cranes that arrive in Bharatpur, and so decided to try their luck with tame human-reared cranes. These they released in the areas of the park where the wild cranes were, hoping that they would make friends and eventually fly away with the wild ones back to Siberia. But alas, a friendship never developed and the wild cranes flew back without taking the tame ones with them.

I saw one of these 'tame' cranes in the park on one of my trips. It had bands on its legs (for identification) and seemed quite happy, rootling about in the marsh all by itself. But it is going to be sad to visit Bharatpur in winter, knowing that you will probably never see wild sibeys there again. (And they winter nowhere else in India.) That used to be the highpoint of most people's visit to the park, and there was always a gaggle of admirers gathered at the spot from where these VIP cranes could be seen. Sure, there is still a large flock of these birds that winter in China, so it's not as though they've become completely extinct or something.

But knowing our destructive and dreadful ways, for how long will they be safe?

It is a bird you tend to see in fields or marshes from the window of a railway carriage, while rollicking through the central, western, eastern and northern plains of India (but alas not in the south). Two birds—usually, one calmly following the other. Tall (around 150 centimetres or 5 feet) stately birds in ash grey, with a naked vivid scarlet head, large bill and orange eyes, stalking sedately through the green paddy, sometimes with an orange-hued youngster in tow.

The sarus crane is our most familiar crane, and a resident of fields, jheels, marshes and well-watered open country. In Sanskrit, its name means 'lake bird' which is so very apt. While you're not very likely to be able to hear its clarion bugle-call above the rattling of the train, if and when you do so, it is a sound that will make you sad and happy at the same time. First, one bird will trumpet hauntingly, as if filled with loneliness, and almost immediately, its partner will answer it and before you know it there is a duet going on and you have goosebumps! And if you see the sarus dance, you'll be hard pressed not to want to join them!

All cranes love to dance. Madly, wildly, crazily, beautifully. They dance when they're happy, when they're in love, when thunder rumbles and great granite clouds pile up, or when they simply feel like it. They may dance in pairs, or whole flocks may dance together. Both partners dance, usually with the male starting the party and inviting the female to follow.

The sarus will first trip around each other, with small stiff steps, wings half open. Suddenly, they'll bounce up exuberantly, wings semi-unfurled, and then bob and bow and cavort and caper, bugling crazily in an excess of high spirits. They'll pick up twigs or stalks of grass and toss these up joyfully, trying to spear them on their way down. Actually, if you watch the sarus (and other cranes) dance, you may be reminded of some of our own folk and tribal dances...

Like other cranes, the sarus is a ground-nester, and breeds between July and December. It will usually choose a raised spot in the middle of a paddyfield (the 'bund' perhaps) or marsh, and set up home here. A bulky mound of vegetation consisting of stalks and reeds and rushes suffices for the nest, and two eggs are laid. Incubation lasts for about a month. Both parents take part in nest-building, incubation and bringing up the young, with the male chiefly concerned with security. About ten weeks after hatching, the 'chick' is ready to fly.

There are no broken marriages or divorces amongst the sarus—they pair for life. In fact, it is said that if one bird dies, its partner pines and starves itself to death. For this devotion, the sarus is much revered by village folk and is never harmed. As a result, it has become quite tame and it is common to see farmers and sarus cranes working together in the same field.

Inspite of this, the number of sarus cranes in India is declining. As usual, we are encroaching rampantly into their territory and pushing them out. Wetlands, marshes, swamps, jheels and riverbanks are being drained and converted by us into agricultural fields. Also, it is feared that the insecticides and fertilisers we use in our fields are additionally responsible for the birds' decline. These poisonous substances are taken in by the adults while feeding on 'contaminated' cereals, and lead to imperfect or unfertile eggs being laid.

Most cranes are vegetarian and do a lot of damage to crops. Wheat is a big favourite with common and demoiselle cranes, as are pods of 'arhar' dal, and groundnut. They also love watermelon, and do a lot of damage by poking them full of holes. Siberian cranes, also largely vegetarian, are more specialised in their eating habits, and relish tubers (fleshy underwater stems) of sedges—which are marsh plants—as well as worms and insects. The sarus prefers non-vegetarian fare, especially fish and frogs and lizards and large insects. But it also has a good appetite for freshly sown cereal crops.

Cranes are high-flying birds and love soaring in huge circles way up in the heavens. They fly with their necks and legs extended to the utmost, and with steady graceful wingbeats. Throughout the world these great birds are getting rarer, and the future for at least some of the fourteen species in the world, does not look very bright. The world will certainly be a poorer and sadder place without these wonderful high-spirited dancers of the marshes, and trumpeters of the skies.

The Spirit of Wildfowl

*W*HISSZHOOOM! WHISSZOOOMZOOMZOOM!

The supersonic sound seems to come from an empty blue sky. From invisible jet fighters streaking through the stratosphere. You stare heavenwards, strangely excited and elated by the whistling. *Whisszhoom! Whisszhoomzhoom!* Then, you spot them. Tiny specks against the blue, arrowing over. Not jet fighters.

Ducks.

Ducks that are now zinging directly overhead. Ducks that are suddenly falling, falling, falling tumbling down down down, rocking and slewing violently from side to side as though out of control. As though all shot up, their wing feathers splayed wide open at the tips. Mayday! Mayday! Mayday!

But no! A few metres above the lake, they miraculously regain complete control. Braking hard with flashing wings, tails flared out, bodies arched gracefully, they touch down with scarcely a sploosh. Wag their tails a bit—as though in approval of a job well done—and start murmuring to each other in that comfortable way ducks have. While your heart still thumps, boom! boom! boom! What a landing! Later you learn that the manouevre—of falling out of the sky with wingtips splayed open—is called whiffling. Whatever it's called, you can only go wow! And wait breathlessly for the next squadron of sizzling whifflers.

At other times they can set a completely different mood. On a buttery winter morning for instance, a flock of two thousand will be dozing on the water, heads-in-wing, fat breasts thrust out soaking in the pale sunshine. Some, those that are awake will be murmuring softly and contentedly—a sound that makes you feel happy and dreamy and at peace with the world. A few clowns in the crowd will upend themselves in the water, and paddling their orange flippers, revolve slowly, their bottoms and tails pointing skywards and rotating like ack-ack guns following targets.

There's an aura of mystery and wonder about ducks and geese and swans. Probably because they're the most well-known and legendary of all migratory birds. When suddenly, five thousand arrive at a lake that till yesterday lay empty and still as a mirror—you can't help shaking your head in wonder, as when huge skeins of geese fly past, in wavy 'V's, conversing with each other, knowing exactly where they're going.

Ducks, geese, and swans as a group are known as wildfowl and there's no mistaking them for any other group of birds. That long flat bill, those brightly coloured flipper-feet, that waddle that

DUCKS
1. Spot-billed Duck, 2. Brahminy Duck or Ruddy Shelduck,
3. Ferruginous Duck, 4. Pintail

makes you giggle, that delightful cheerful wag of the tail, and that hoarse motor-horn quack-quack *quaaack!* All that (and more) is specialist equipment of course, designed for their special way of life. A life that is spent almost entirely on water.

Take the bill for example. Both the upper and lower parts (mandibles) are equipped with comb-like filtration plates which strain minute animal and vegetable matter out of the water. The water is sucked in, and expelled from the mouth by the tongue which acts like a piston (remember the flamingos?). The brightly coloured feet are webbed between the front toes, and hitched right at the back of the bird to assist it to propel itself in the water. (Just as a ship's propellers are located right at the back of the ship.) The wings are sleek and narrow and pointed, designed for high-speed long-distance flying. As for the motor-horn *quaack!*—that I guess is to make us laugh.

For centuries they've been symbols of wild and lonely places—which is why they're called wildfowl. And yet, for centuries they've been domesticated by us. They've been shot in the millions by hunters all over the world and have become skilled in avoiding guns. The Keoladeo National Park in Bharatpur for example, was actually designed as the wildfowl hunting preserve of the Maharaja of Bharatpur, before Salim Ali urged it be put to better use.

Even today, they are not spared in most parts of the country. Shikaris lie in wait for them on the reedy fringes of jheels and lakes, swamps and marshes, rivers and tanks. Many bird sanctuaries too are not safe. Thousands are shot and trapped at Chilka lake in Orissa for example, and a few years ago there was a horrific report that you could buy a duck for thirty bucks at Harike Wildlife Sanctuary in Punjab. There is nothing 'sporting' about the way they are killed either. It's all so that poachers can make money, and the rich and elite can boast that they can offer you duck at their dining tables.

Most of our ducks are migratory and start arriving in jheels and rivers and swamps and talaos from August onwards. Here they will stay till March or April, before setting off for the 5,000 to 6,000 kilometre flight back to the wilds of Central Asia and Siberia, where they will breed. Places like the Keoladeo in Bharatpur, Chilka in Orissa and Point Calimere in Tamil Nadu are well-known for the vast flocks they attract, but nearly every large water-body in the country will have its share of wildfowl during winter. Even small village talaos and tanks will have their visitors from afar.

Most species of ducks, geese and swans nest in the colder, northern parts of the globe, many near the freezing Arctic circle. As a rule they're ground nesters and their fluffy, downy chicks are born well-prepared for life: they can waddle and swim right-away. Many species of duck moult, or shed, all their flight feathers together for a period of three or four weeks in a year. Now they cannot fly, and must lie low. They make their feathers waterproof by applying oil on them while preening, from a special gland near the base of the tail.

In their efforts to sort out and classify them, scientists have broadly divided them into ten tribes, which belong to two broad groups. One group, the Anserinae, has the swans and geese and whistling ducks (which are duck-like geese!). The other group, the Anatidae, has the seven tribes of 'proper' and 'typical' duckie-ducks. Of the approximately one hundred and forty-five types or species of wildfowl in the world, we in India have recorded forty, most of which as I mentioned earlier, are migratory.

In India, swans are very seldom seen and of the six or seven types of geese that have been recorded, only two—the barheaded and greylag—are common. The duck-which-is-like-a-goose is the whistling teal, a charming bird with a lovely enchanting flying whistle.

In the proper, typical duckie-duck family, there are seven tribes of which four are found in India.

The Dipping Ducks: This is the biggest tribe of them all. On their wings, members sport a bright badge of identification; a patch of glittering feathers that are either metallic green or blue, often striped or splotched with white. This patch is called the speculum. Each species in this tribe has its specially coloured speculum, which serves as a sort of visual password, and ensures that the bird interacts and mates only with its own kind. Dipping ducks, or dabblers as they are also known, are usually handsomely patterned, and the males are usually brightly coloured. The females are usually drab, splotched and dappled in various shades of brown and biscuit. Dabblers do headstands in the water and feed just beneath the surface, chiefly on minute vegetable and animal matter. They can also do near vertical missile-like take-offs from the water.

The Diving Ducks: This tribe contains species of rather drab-coloured ducks, who keep together in colossal flocks. They are also known as pochards. They have short, rather heavy bodies and lack the bright speculum on the wings that the dippers have. Their legs are placed very wide apart, and farther back than that of the dippers (which makes them waddle even more hilariously) and they have a flap on the hind toe (which the dippers don't) to help them dive. Pochards dive deep to the bottom of jheels and talaos, and filter their food, animal and vegetable matter, from the mud and ooze. Actually, the presence of pochards on a water body is an indication that the water here is quite deep. Pochards run pitter-patter over the surface of the water before taking off.

Tree Ducks or Perching Ducks: A small tribe, members of which spend more time up in the trees (and nest in hollows) than those of any other tribe. They have strong claws which are long and sharp to help them clamber up the trees. Both the male and the female are alike.

Shelducks: This tribe consists of big, brightly-coloured ducks with short, thick bills. They're rather quarrelsome by nature. In fact, the female usually provokes two males into fighting over her, and then chooses the victor as her mate.

Let us now meet some of the more common members of these various tribes.

DIPPING DUCKS

The Common Teal: This little duck wears a broad silky green mask across its eyes. The mask is bordered with white and makes the bird look as though it's all dressed up for a costume party.

Its head is a shiny russet—an orangey-brown—and its body is greyish, with fine wavy pencil markings. The speculum is black and green and caramel coloured and is easily visible when the bird flies. The female is mottled dark and light brown and has a black and green speculum.

Common teals are amongst our most numerous of migratory waterfowl. I've always found them very shy and wary—even the ones that winter in the ponds at the Delhi zoo, along with other ducks. If they see you looking at them, they'll glide away furtively, heads sunk low into their shoulders.

The Pintail: This is one of my favourites and a real smart one too. It is 'normal' duck size, and has a fine upright carriage in the water. The head is dark, chocolate-brown with two white stripes running down into the white neck, like icing. The body is a beautiful silver-grey with a finely pencilled wave-like pattern. The speculum is metallic bronze-green. The bird gets its name from the long, pointed antennae-like feathers that stick out of its tail. The pintail is capable of amazing vertical take-offs from the water. They are amongst the most common and numerous of our migratory ducks. Those that come to the Delhi zoo are not shy at all and will happily swim to within a few feet of you, especially if it's near their feeding time.

The female is quite attractively patterned in dark and golden brown.

The Shoveller: This one looks like a lean-mean-quacking machine! Actually that's because it has a somewhat hunched posture in the water, and that in turn is because of the way it feeds. Its most prominent feature is its broad black shovel or spatula shaped bill (which I think looks like the top half of a patent leather slipper!). Craning its neck and bill stiffly out in front, the shoveller paddles forth. The lower half of its bill slices just through the water, and the top half, is at water level. Minute animal matter is filtered out by the comb like edges of the bill. Of course, the shoveller can also headstand in the water and show off its bright orange paddling flippers. It will then right itself and glare at you for laughing at it.

Even otherwise it's a fine looking duck. The head is metallic green, but can look a royal purple depending on how the light falls on it. The breast is whiter than what the best detergent can ever produce. There is a lovely flame-blue patch on the front part of the wing, which is separated from the metallic green speculum by a white bar. The body and underparts of the bird are russet. The female, as usual, is splotched in light and dark brown.

The Wigeon: Another smartly turned out duck, this one. Overall it's silvery grey, but has a russet coloured head with a condensed milk coloured patch on the forehead. The breast is silvery pink. The bill, which is small in comparison to the

WIGEON

shoveller's, is blue-grey. There is a white patch on the folded wing and the speculum is green, finely bordered with black. The female is dark brown, mottled with light brown.

Wigeons aren't as common perhaps as pintails and shovellers and common teals, but it is well worth looking out for these neatly dressed fellows in a crowd of the others.

Gadwall: Another very common migrant to the northern parts of the country, though less common in the central and southern areas. They are dark-brown and grey ducks, with coal-black near the tail and an attractive russet patch on the wing, just in front of the black and white speculum. Their legs and feet are yellow. The female, as usual, is dark-brown, dappled with buff. While flying you can identify them by the flashing white speculum which often disappears when the bird sits on the water.

The Gargeny or Blue-winged Teal: Along with the common teal, this one too is a very early arrival. I remember being bamboozled by a flock of them over a period of two or three winters at Sultanpur jheel where they used to turn up in early September. I didn't know what the heck they were, because they were still in 'eclipse' plumage, which is the dress they put on for a short while immediately after moulting, and which makes the males look like females! The females, in turn, are quite difficult to identify and easy to confuse with common teals. Thankfully, there were some who had changed into their proper male attire and that eventually solved my problem. Their most conspicuous feature is their prominent shaggy looking white eyebrows— which makes them look rather like grandfather ducks! Their heads are pinkish-brown and speckled, their underparts dark pepper-brown and patterned—or scalloped—with light brown. The wings are a lovely shade of blue-grey and the speculum is green, bordered with two white bands.

The female, as I mentioned earlier, looks a lot like the female of the common teal, and here, the speculum plays a vital role in identifying her. It's green and white for the gargeny, as against black and green for the common teal. Gargenys are found on water bodies throughout the country in winter.

The Mallard: The great ancestor of all our domestic ducks so this one deserves respect. Quack-quack-quack! It is therefore thought to be the most 'typical' of ducks, though I wonder what all the other ducks think about that. It has a big emerald green head and two curly-wurly feathers sticking out of its bottom, which I think look like kiss curls. Its body is largely grey, with fine black wavy pencil lines. The breast is russet and the bird wears a white collar at the throat. The speculum is violet-purple, bordered with black and white lines. The bill is yellow, the legs bright orange.

The female is brown and buff, spotted and streaked with black.

The Spotbill: A resident duck that is found all over India. It is fairly large, and its scaly patterned plumage is light-and-dark brown. Its dark bill has a yellow tip and there are two orange 'bindis' at its base—one on either side of the forehead. The speculum is metallic green and white. The feet are bright orange. Both male and female are alike.

This dark-eyed duck breeds during the monsoons, between July and September, laying six to twelve eggs in a pad of weeds and grass on the margins of water bodies.

DIVING DUCKS

As pochards are ducks that like deep water, they are usually to be found swimming far away in the middle of a large lake or tank or river. You usually need a powerful pair of binoculars to see them properly. Also, some of them tend to float rather low in the water, and often disappear completely behind the waves.

The Common Pochard: Of the three kinds of pochards we shall meet here, the common pochard looks a bit like a businessman. He has a ginger-coloured head and is clad in sober grey and black business-suit. His breast, and the top of his back are black as are the rump and the feathers covering the tail. The rest of the plumage is greyish-brown and finely woven. His wife is greyish-brown too, but of a more faded shade than her husband. She has a ruff-like neck, breast and upper back.

Common pochards keep together in huge rafts on large and deep water bodies. They arrive by around the end of October

COMMON POCHARDS

and stay on till the end of March. They are common in north India, but get rather rare as you go south. I've seen enormous numbers of them bobbing quietly together in the Jamuna at Delhi, as well as at Badkhal lake, which is just outside the city. They seem to be rather shy, quiet characters, who mind their own business and would like you to mind your own.

TUFTED POCHARDS

The Tufted Pochard: If the common pochard is dressed like a businessman, the tufted pochard is dressed like a politician on Republic Day! He is formally turned out in a black 'bandh-galla' Nehru jacket, and a spotless white kurta, and his glistening black 'shendi' is well-oiled and slicked down. Also, he has these harsh golden-yellow eyes that glare at you sternly and make you wonder if he has ever had any fun in his life. Certainly he looks as though he doesn't want you to have any fun either!

Actually, he is very smart. The head, neck, breast, back and tail are jet black, the sides of the body and flanks, spotless white. A slick black shendi (or occipital crest) lies limply along the back of the head, but makes you giggle when the wind tugs it this way and that. Such a spruced up, formal looking fellow, having his hairdo all messed up! Delightful! In flight, a white wing 'mirror' is prominently visible.

The female is dark brown in the places where the male is black, and sooty where he is white. Poor thing!

Tufted pochards arrive in mid-October and stay on till the end of March. They are common in north India but rarer in the south.

The Red-crested Pochard: I've left the best pochard for last! This one is dressed like a very fashion-conscious and avant-garde—or modern—artist who will charge many lakhs of rupees for a painting you cannot make head or tail of. People usually look weird when they dress like this (and behave that way too) but this pochard looks absolutely stunning.

His mop of silky hair on the top of his square cut head, is a bright henna—or mehandi—colour. It does look as though he has just dyed it rather virulently. He also looks as though he's applied a thick, glistening layer of bright crimson lipstick on his bill! He wears a black polo-neck, and brown and white outfit and swims about looking very pleased with himself. (The head is a flaming carrot colour, the breast and undersides are black, the back light-brown, the flanks are white as are the wing patches.) His wife, poor dear, is clad in dull shawl-browns, probably embarrassed by her husband's outrageous attire. But these are easily my most favourite pochards.

The red-crested pochard arrives in October and is gone by mid-March, but you can enjoy its company in deep water bodies nearly throughout the country.

Much to my delight I found all of the above three swimming around in brisk bobbing circles in Badkhal lake one winter. The common pochards behaved a bit furtively, keeping low in the water and hiding behind the waves; the tufted pochards looked stern and stiff and strict as though they were on their way to receive Padmashree awards from the president; the red-crested pochards sat on top of the waves and paddled about gaily without a care in the world. Occasionally, they would dive beneath and then pop up suddenly like a cork does when held underwater and then released.

TREE DUCKS

Quack! Quack! QuackyDuck!:

I used to think that whoever had named this sad-looking little black-and-white thing 'Quacky-duck', had completely run out of ideas. But there is a reason behind this ridiculous name: the bird apparently actually cackles 'quack! quack! quacky-duck!' as it whirrs swiftly away. Or so I've read...Because some of the other sharp staccato calls of this little fellow have been described as 'car-car-carwack!' and (by a British ornithologist who was also a colonel), 'fix-bayonets! fix-bayonets!'

Anyway, the poor Quacky-duck also has two other more respectable names: the cotton teal or the cotton pygmy goose.

It's the smallest of all ducks in the world and has a stubby goose-like bill. The male wears a neat black cap on a white head, and a broad black collar at the base of his throat. The back is black, with a metallic greenish and purplish sheen. When it flies—low and twistingly—a broad white bar on the black wings is very noticeable. The female is more dull and brown and has a dark line through the eye.

Cotton teals are resident ducks and nest between May and September in the hollows of tree trunks, of trees usually standing in water. Six to fourteen eggs may be laid (by more than one female) in a single nest. They're mainly vegetarian and can be found in water bodies nearly all over the country.

The Comb Duck or Nakta: At first glance, this one looks like a jumbo-sized cotton teal, because it has much the same colour and pattern as the tiny-tot. But it also looks as though it's been spattered with black ink or paint—and sure enough, the male even seems to carry what looks like an ink bottle on his bill! Actually, that's the so-called 'comb' and apparently serves to impress the females and probably warn off other males during the breeding season. This big goose-like duck has a black back glossed with purple and green, and matching wings. Its sides are greyish. Females are smaller, not as glossy and don't carry the inkpot.

Naktas are resident ducks and nest in the hollows of old trees, between June and September. They're found all over India. I see them regularly at the Delhi Zoo but haven't been able to find out if they nest there. Normally, between seven and fifteen eggs are laid, though in one case forty-seven eggs were found in a single hollow. They were probably laid by several females possibly due to a shortage of hollows. As ducklings can forage for themselves as soon as they hatch—the parents, or foster parents—as the case may have been, would not really have had a problem rearing the chicks. Otherwise, just imagine if you had forty-seven hungry mouths to feed! Naktas are rather silent ducks and may only croak with annoyance if you disturb them and force them to fly off.

SHELDUCKS

The Legend of the Brahminy Ducks: Once upon a time, there were two young Brahmins who fell in love. Their parents, and all the village elders however, frowned upon this relationship. It was not right, they thought, that two young people should decide on their own to fall in love and marry. So they forbade the two from meeting each other. But meet the two lovers did, and for this crime were turned into a pair of brahminy ducks. They were doomed thus, to remain within sight and hearing of one another, but ever separated by a wide river... And to this day, Chawka and Chawki, the two lovers, call to one another across the water: 'Chawka aanga?' ('Chawka, shall I come?'), which is answered sadly, 'Chawki na aao!' ('Chawki, don't come!') because the punishment is still in force.

You must be wondering why they were doomed thus to remain within sight and hearing of each other and yet separated just because they were turned into a pair of brahminy ducks. Well, the legend has arisen (but the details of which I've just made up!) out of the habit of brahminy duck pairs to separate widely from one another while feeding at a riverbank or lakeside. And equally, by their rather clanging and nasal sounding *aan-aang* calls, which have been turned into 'Chawka aanga?' and 'Chawki na-aao!' in the story.

These big handsome ducks, also called ruddy shelducks, are the colour of burnt sugar, a glowing orange-brown. Their heads are paler, almost creamish, and their wings are beautiful—white, black and bottle green.

Brahminy ducks are winter visitors throughout the country (between October and April) and can usually be spotted in small numbers on the sandbanks of wide rivers, or the edges of large, open lakes. They breed in the mountains of Ladakh, at a height of over 4,000 metres above sea level, in May and June. A thick pad of white down (the birds' own) is stuffed into fissures or holes in mountain cliffsides. In Ladakh, they're very friendly with the local Buddhist population, who never harm them, and may even stroll and graze on the rooftops of the villagers' houses. But when they visit the rest of India during the winter, they are amongst the most wary of ducks and the first to fly away. It doesn't say much for the rest of us, does it?

Despite the legend, brahminy ducks are, true to their tribe (the shelducks) rather quarrelsome creatures who don't like mixing too much with others, or even their own kind. But there are always exceptions, and there have been reports that many thousand strong have been seen on Chilka lake in Orissa. They are omnivorous and eat grains, tubers, insects, shoots, small aquatic creatures and reptiles.

WHISTLING-DUCKS

Lesser Whistling Teal: They can stop you dead in your tracks. As you amble along a reed-fringed jheel or tank, their lovely piping *whi-whee! whi-whee! seasick-seasick!* whistles will startle you to a halt and quickly make you smile. Just who is whistling at you in that cheeky yet charming way?! Well, if you turn around quick enough, you will see a flock of small golden-brown ducks flying hurriedly by in a large circle, and looking—judging by the feeble yet frantic way they flap their wings—as though they're all about to crash land in the water. Sure enough, still whistling cheerfully, they lose height and skimming over the water, sploosh to a relieved landing, and vanish amidst the floating vegetation. Lesser whistling teals or now recently renamed, lesser whistling ducks!

You'll have to stand quietly and patiently on the bank or bundh of the water body if you want to see them on the water because they are as shy as they are charming. They'll keep near the reeds and rarely will venture out into open water. They're small—or as the French would say—petite ducks, toast-brown with a maroon tinge to their plumage. They have a happy, perky attitude and somehow, always make me think that they've just all had a crew-cut.

Lesser whistling ducks are resident all over the country and keep together in small flocks. They like vegetation covered water bodies, though they are happy to perch in trees too. In fact, they nest in the hollows of old trees—between June and October— or sometimes take over the unused nests of crows, vultures and herons. Between seven and twelve eggs may be laid and incubation lasts about a month.

They are cautious ducks and feed at night, mostly on vegetarian fare. I find them really enchanting and am delighted to meet up with them on my trips to the Keoladeo in Bharatpur. There's really nothing to beat ending a day's birding by watching these happy sounding ducks give you a cheerful whistling flypast.

Lesser whistling ducks have a big brother—the large whistling teal or large fulvous duck. Apart from being larger, these have creamish-white feathers at the base of the tail, as against the smaller brother's chestnut coloured ones. Also, they wear a smudged rusty white collar round the foreneck. Large fulvous ducks are much more scarce than their smaller brothers, so not seen very often.

Goosebumps with Wild Geese

LIKE A SOFT ACRID CLOUD, SMELLING STRANGELY OF gunpowder, the fog muffled the world, around us. We could hardly see beyond our rosy frozen noses, as we trundled slowly down the path. On either side Bharatpur's marshy jheels spread, in which we knew, wildfowl aplenty rested. Suddenly, from somewhere above, an unmistakable and unforgettable call drew close.

Aahg-ung-ung! Aahng-ung-ung!

The honking of wild geese! It was a sound that always thrilled one in a strange goosebumpy way...

Even in this cottonwool murk, in which no plane dare fly, they were taking flight. Dimly we saw their ghostly shapes wing whooshingly past us, looming out of the fog for an instant, then vanishing. Flying in perfect 'V' formation. Obviously, they circled the marsh and then we heard them splash-land and begin to converse peaceably, *gag-gag-gag!* as though this were the most perfect day for flying!

And indeed, on one such day, in another jheel far away (at Sultanpur near Delhi) I watched, equally fascinated, as a squadron of barheaded geese approached for landing. They flew steadily over the lake, and then banked around in formation, showing off their striking grey, black and white plumage beautifully against the dark green foliage of the trees. Suddenly, a few birds side slipped, and dropped like they were shot, before righting themselves and touching down on the water. The rest of the squadron continued to bank and circle and landed one by one, in a more sober and normal way.

Both these species of geese, the greylag and the barheaded, are migratory and may fly right over the Himalayas and even the Everest on their journeys. The greylag is a big brown and grey goose, with a well patterned plumage and pink legs and bill. The barheaded is smaller and more graceful, dressed in silvery-grey, black and white. It has two charcoal-like markings across the back of its head and a white stripe down each side of its grey neck. Its legs and bill are orange-yellow.

While the greylag winters chiefly in north India and is not found in south India or the central areas, the barheaded is found on large water bodies nearly throughout the country. Both species are extraordinarily wary, because they're shot everywhere by hunters. They are also extremely fond of the fresh shoots of winter crops, which makes them enemies of the farmer. They feed in fields all night, grazing on leaves and tender shoots. A goose is said to be able to pick a hundred tender leaves of grass in a minute. Come daybreak, and they'll take-off with a rush of beating wings, for some large jheel or river. Here they will doze peacefully, head buried in the feathers of the back, all day. But yes, there are always sentries posted and at the first signs of danger they'll be up and off.

The greylag breeds in faraway Central Asia and Siberia, whereas some barheaded geese breed in the high mountain lakes of Ladakh. The nest is a well-padded depression in the ground in which three to six eggs are laid. The mother does most of the incubation which lasts for about a month, while the gander vigorously protects the fuzzy gooselings from danger.

Monster of the Gloom

BEWARE! IT IS DUSK ON A GLOOMY MONSOON EVENING ON the Ridge. You are late for your walk and quicken your footsteps as you pass the dank weedy pond, fringed with umbrella plants. This is no place to linger after dusk. Sweat prickles at the back of your neck and your hands are clammy. And well, may they be!

Krr...kwak! Krr...Kwak-kwak-kwaak! Krr...Kwak-Kwak-Kwak! Kook-Kook-Kook!

It's hoarse. It's loud. It's wild. It's monstrous! It's scaring the pants off you! And obviously it's seen you!

What is this monster of the gloom giving tongue thus, and making you feel an urgent need for the bathroom? Hairy, long-fanged, well-clawed, lava-eyed and large as a bear no doubt! And twice as dangerous. Maybe even a dreadful morphed creature of the twenty-first century!

And what is that neat hunch-backed grey bird, striding down the path ahead, jerking a rusty-brown tail up-and-down at you? About the size of a small hen, friendly-looking, slaty grey, with long greenish legs and large feet. As it stops and turns, you see that its face and breast are chalk-white. It stomps hurriedly into the reeds and vanishes. And then...

Krr...kwak-kwak! Krr...Kwaak! Kwaak! Krr...Kwaak! Kwaak!

And if you remain here, you can hear it all night. Sweet dreams!

But yes indeed, that is the whitebreasted waterhen giving tongue; the same neat, friendly fellow that just vanished, flicking its rusty rump at you.

Normally, a shy and silent bird, it tends to get rather excited in its breeding season which is between June and October. Normally, you wouldn't imagine that such a well-behaved looking bird could make such a monstrous noise. I mean, the bird lives a quiet, peaceful life, skulking around the fringes o ponds and lakes and water bodies, all over India. It is even foun in parks in large towns, which means it's pretty civilised by ou standards. It pecks harmlessly at insects, shoots of marsh-plants grain and stuff like that. It nests on the ground, or just above i a bush, building a shallow cup with twigs and creeper stems Both parents bring up six to seven perfectly delightful fuzzy wuzzy all-black chicks. And yet, when June comes along, it wil fly up to a well-hidden perch, where it can see you, and giv tongue. Scaring the daylights out of you yet again.

P.S.: The loud throaty call is probably to scare away all other male waterhens from the area, let alone everyone else! And perhaps, also to attract females. Though I wonder about that...

The Hanky Waver

ACTUALLY, THIS DUSKY, DARK GREY AND BROWN BIRD doesn't like being seen. So generally, it skulks along the edges of reed-fringed ponds, bobbing its head as if it were trying to duck out of view. Unfortunately, it has what looks like a small white handkerchief pinned to the bottom of its tail which flicks up and down as the head bobs. So suddenly, you begin to wonder, who is wavng a little hanky at you amidst the reeds and bullrushes? And the poor moorhen's cover is blown!

Also, the moorhen likes swimming, so if you catch it paddling about in the middle of a pond you can get a good look at it. About the size of a small hen (let's say a Made in Japan hen!), it is dusky grey and brown all over with a white streak where the wings fold into the body. It has a bright red frontal shield on its forehead, just in front of its greenish bill. (These frontal shields always remind me of helmets worn by amateur boxers.) Even in the water, the moorhen swims in an earnest, bobbing fashion, and waves its little white hanky at you. Once it comes ashore, you'll see its longish green legs and enormous splayed-out feet, so useful for balancing on wobbly water plants.

Moorhens are resident birds, but the local population is joined by many more who migrate here in winter. They fly in a very alarming manner—usually fast and low over the water, in a dead straight line, with rapid flurrying wingbeats. The head is stretched out ahead (as though wanting to reach safety as quickly as possible), the legs trail behind. They remind me of planes in trouble. But the birds must be good fliers—they do after

INDIAN MOORHENS
1. Adult, 2. Juvenile

all, fly huge distances at great heights on their migratory journeys. The birds feed on insects, grain, and shoots—much the same stuff as the waterhen. Their calls however, are nowhere as scary: a sharp cracky *Kirrik-creak-rek-rek*, emitted usually in the mornings or evenings and when they are safely hidden from view.

Moorhens breed between June and September, building bulky nests out of reeds and sedges either on the ground or on a low shrub, close to water. Between seven and twelve eggs are laid. The chicks, who will chirrup even while in the egg, recognise their parents' voices and will shut up immediately when their parents warn them. One explanation given for the hanky waving habit, is that it enables the chicks to follow their parents easily—both on land or in the water—by attracting their attention. Otherwise we might just have a lot of little fuzzy black moorhen chicks wandering about lost and forlorn in our ponds.

Kickboxers in the Swamps

QUITE HONESTLY, PURPLE SWAMPHENS (OR PURPLE moorhens as they were earlier called) look as though they've been designed for kick-boxing in the swamps. These big bulky birds are a beautiful greeny-purplish blue—the three hues merging shimmeringly together. Their huge domed forehead is protected by a large pillar-box red frontal shield (or casque) and a stout bill. And their long red legs have size thirteen feet. They look like cushions standing on stilts. Under their tail, which is flicked up with every stride, these muscular hefties have what look like a couple of puffy white clouds stuck on side by side, which makes them look absolutely hilarious.

Purple swamphens stride jerkily about on the edges of marshes and jheels, in pairs or small groups, all over the country. Their plumage can camouflage them extremely well, but happily, they draw attention to themselves by their querulous noisy calls and diabolical sounding 'heh-heh!' laughter. I once watched a group feeding in the marshes of the Keoladeo National Park: they simply would not let one another feed in peace. If one bird discovered a juicy titbit—a tuber perhaps, and upended excitedly trying to reach it, the others would immediately stop what they were doing and stomp over, cackling harshly. They would try and shove the finder and each other out of the way and grab the titbit, and you would see all these puffy cottonwool clouds bobbing up and down on the surface of the marsh. I really expected a ferocious bout of kick-boxing to break out and was a little disappointed when this didn't happen.

The birds breed between April and September. Before doing so, the male offers water-weeds to his sweetheart as a gift. He holds them in his beak like a bouquet of flowers, and bowing low before her chuckles proudly. (And up goes the cloud bottom again!) Later, a large pad of reed stems and leaves (called 'flags') are interwoven together on floating matter, just above water level. Three to seven eggs are laid. When danger threatens the chicks, they sink completely under water, with only the top part of their bill breaking the surface.

PURPLE SWAMPHEN

Don't be a Greedy (or Silly) Coot!

SEEN FROM A DISTANCE, SWIMMING ABOUT IN THE WATER, you can easily mistake coots for ducks. But coots are coots and don't have the typical flat duck bill; their bills are a pale translucent pinkish-white and pointed, and go well with the chalk-white frontal shield they have on their foreheads. They are dumpy looking charcoal black birds, about the size of a plump chicken, with no tail to speak of and rather oversized dull green feet and legs. They love each other's company and swim together in large groups.

Coots are resident as well as migratory. In winter, huge swarms settle on water bodies all over the country, especially in the northern parts. They consume aquatic insects, shoots, weeds and squishy things living in the water and mud, in search of which they can dive deep. In turn, they are hunted by eagles and harriers—and as we have seen, blacknecked storks.

Coots appear to have a hard time getting off from the water. They'll skitter splashily across the surface, beating their wings into a blur, and scampering madly on those oversized feet. When about a thousand of them do this at the same time (which is what they seem to like doing) it sounds like some gigantic ogre is vigorously rinsing his mouth—after eating coots perhaps, which didn't taste very good! But the noise is frightening enough to distract a hunting eagle or harrier from its target. Coots have a rather loud and clear trumpet-like call, and as they like remaining awake all night—feeding—they often blow their trumpets at this time.

COOT
1. Adult, 2. Juvenile

Resident coots nest between July and September in the north, and in November–December in the south. A large mass of rushes is put together amongst the reeds, just above the water level. Between six and ten eggs are laid and incubated by both parents for about three weeks.

Being a greedy young coot can be both silly and dangerous. Unlike the parents of other bird-chicks, like the purple heron we met earlier, coot parents ensure that all their chicks get an equal share of the food. A chick who is unnecessarily greedy is severely disciplined by its parent: it is picked up and shaken vigorously, or given a royal ducking. Often, the poor chick is so shocked by this treatment that it hides away in the rushes and reeds— and sadly, may lose its family forever—as they drift away. Certainly, it doesn't pay to be a greedy coot.

Spider's Legs on Lily Pads

*I*MAGINE YOU ARE FLOATING ON YOUR BACK IN A BEAUTIFUL lily pond. The waxy pale yellow and mauve blooms float placidly alongside you on their raft of leaves. Above, a dark-grey monsoon sky broods and rumbles to itself. All around, it is vibrantly green, and just next to your ear, a bright golden bullfrog grins and goes *berrek! berrek!*

Then there's a light, spiky spidery touch on your stomach. Another on your chest. And then one on your face... Covering it, and lightly, so lightly pushing you under... With a scream you explode into wakefulness as the frog plops headlong into the water. You've been dreaming about jacanas again! Those beautiful, spider-footed birds also known as lily trotters.

Actually, I'll never forget the first time I saw pheasant-tailed jacanas. (No, I wasn't floating on a lily pond!) It was near Rajghat, on a grey and green monsoon day. The fields around

Rajghat glimmered with silver-brown rainwater ponds. Then suddenly a pealing, high-pitched *mee-e-ou, mee-e-ou*; call rang out—a musical mewing in the wind and a pair of birds flew hastily across, in front of me. Chocolate-brown and white, wit¹ beautiful lemon-gold on the back of the head and nape, and a long delicate curving tail—like that of some exotic princely pheasant. They flew in tandem, calling out to one another, their white wings dazzling, and then landed in the high grass and vanished. It was difficult spotting them again, as they stepped lightly over the lily pads on their enormous spidery feet—for which reason they are called lily-trotters. Their long wire-like toes and nails help them distribute their weight over the lily leaves. These lovely birds wear their elegant scimitar-like tails only in the breeding season—between June and September— and during the rest of the year, are a pale brown and white, with a white necklace on the upper part of the breast. Males and females are alike.

Pheasant-tailed jacanas are found on vegetation covered ponds and water bodies all over the country, and often become quite tame in village tanks and talaos. As do other types of jacanas, they have a sharp spur on the bend of the wing, which some ornithologists say is used for fighting, and others say, is not used for this purpose.

The pheasant-tailed jacana's cousin, the bronze-winged jacana is not perhaps as elegant, but is beautifully coloured. In shape it looks a bit like a moorhen but its neck and breast and face are velvety-black. It has a heavy, snow-white eyebrow which makes it look as though it's wearing a turban with tassles. In the

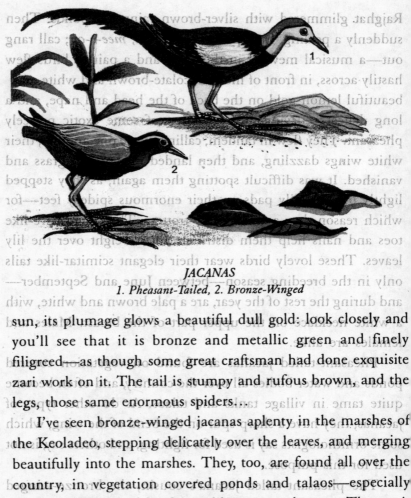

JACANAS
1. Pheasant-Tailed, 2. Bronze-Winged

sun, its plumage glows a beautiful dull gold: look closely and you'll see that it is bronze and metallic green and finely filigreed—as though some great craftsman had done exquisite zari work on it. The tail is stumpy and rufous brown, and the legs, those same enormous spiders....

I've seen bronze-winged jacanas aplenty in the marshes of the Keoladeo, stepping delicately over the leaves, and merging beautifully into the marshes. They, too, are found all over the country, in vegetation covered ponds and talaos—especially those with floating rafts of water lily or water chestnut. They emit a piping *seek-seek-seek*! alarm call and make a lot of noise during the breeding season—again between June and September. Both these species feed on aquatic vegetation and insects and molluscs.

The female jacana is polyandrous—that is, she takes on a number of partners. The male first fights rivals for territory, and having won one, attracts a female. He then builds the nest which is a pad of leaves and weed stems placed almost at water level. In this, the female lays between three and seven eggs (usually four for the bronze-winged jacana). Then she trips off to find another husband for herself leaving the male to incubate the eggs and bring up the family by himself. It was once found, that one female jacana had laid nine clutches—or lots—of eggs in nine different nests.

Black Stilettos and Pink Knitting-Needles

'LOOK!' I SAID POINTING OUT TO THE NEAT BLACK-AND-white bird squatting in the tall grass. 'That blackwinged stilt has got a nest there and is sitting on its eggs!' The bird looked in our direction and uttered a nervous *klek-klek-klek*! Then it rose to its feet and we stared at it in surprise. Its poker-thin pink knitting-needle like legs were the length of a foot-ruler—quite literally making it look as though it were standing on stilts. (Well, what did you expect—it was a stilt after all!) Actually, you normally see the stilt wading about in water—often tummy deep—so you don't get a true idea of its basketball-player height. Its small round head was white, with some peppery smudges—which I knew, sometimes could be more extensive and make the bird look as though it had got a whopping black eye! Its slim body was also white, and its sharp-pointed triangular wings were glossy black with a silky inky tint. This was probably a male then, because the female was more brownish-black than inky-black. The bill was a sharp slim black stiletto.

But what the stilt now did surprised me even more. It ran forward stiffly a few paces, and then settled down in the grass again, still looking at us out of its ruby eyes, as though hoping we were keeping track of it.

'Hey! And look, it's got another nest there!' I exclaimed, not really thinking. Four times the bird rose and settled in different places and of course by now, we realised what it was trying to do. It was trying to deceive us about the true location of its nest and eggs, or perhaps chicks. Actually, chicks—because as I found out later, stilts don't make their nests in grassy fields.

BLACKWINGED STILT

Then, a stray dog who had been accompanying us (and who obviously thought he was the Honorary Wildlife Warden of the Sultanpur National Park where we were) trotted forth to investigate. Immediately the stilt uttered a shrill, panic-stricken *kip-kip-kip*! and stood up, unfurling its angular wings. Then it suddenly drooped one wing to the ground and staggered away, dragging it along the grass and limping. This was, of course, the famous 'broken wing' display that so many parent birds perform in order to lead a predator away from their eggs or chicks. The stilt probably had three or four downy chicks lying doggo in the grass and was trying to make sure that none of us got anywhere close to them.

But while it may be easy to hide your downy chicks in the grass, it's not so easy to hide your nest. Especially when your nest is a mound of reed flags and plant matter arranged higgledy-piggledy together on a bare, clayey lake edge with nothing else in sight. Actually, if you're especially dumb, you might think that it's flotsam and jetsam thrown up on the lake shore—but well, you have to be especially dumb! Because as you walk towards it, you'll be subject to a shrill, piping dive-bombing attack by the parent birds, now screaming *kip-kip-kip*! at you with hysterical anger. They'll flutter all around you, gain height, and with wings sharply angled, zoom down… Watch it, those stiletto bills are like kebab-skewers, and the birds mean business! And you certainly don't want to be a kebab!

Blackwinged stilts are one of our most common water birds and can be found on all kinds of water bodies (even saline ones) throughout the country. Their long legs enable them to wade into water deeper than what most other wading birds can, and so reach food—aquatic insects, molluscs and such succulent stuff—from depths that other birds can't reach. This reduces the competition for food from the others who may like the same kind of stuff. Too bad, those shorties just can't get at them!

Stilts like their own company and remain in flocks of around twenty to hundred birds—when they're not nesting. They spend their time feeding—often with their heads completely submerged and tails pointing skywards (like ducks)—or standing about on one leg, probably day-dreaming. While wading through the water, they are careful to pull up each leg completely clear of the water before moving it forward in the air and then lowering it back into the water. If they tried to push those terribly thin and fragile legs through the water (like we do while wading) they'd probably snap like toothpicks.

The birds fly swiftly, often low over the water, like arrowheads, keeping in touch with their piping, musical calls. They adjust their speed by raising or lowering their legs and land by gliding smoothly down on stiffly held horizontal wings. At the last moment, the long legs are lowered and the bird touches down with a hop and a skip. Sometimes the bird brakes, hovers in mid-air, dangles down its legs and drops down vertically like a helicopter.

Stilts are both resident as well as migratory. While they seem to prefer the water bodies in north India for breeding (between April and August) they spread south in the winter. Usually, four eggs are laid and both parents share incubation—changing places approximately every hour—for between three weeks and a month. Their chicks are terrifically independent right from the start and are *never* fed, let alone spoonfed, by their parents. No running after them with a bowl of slugs, yelling, 'Come on now, eat up your slugs, they're good for you!'

My Most Elegant Wader in the Country

WHENEVER I SPOT A FLOCK OF THEM ON A WATER BODY, I tend to forget about all the other ducks and waders that may also be present, and just stare at them for, my own personal award for the 'Most Elegant Wader in the Country' belongs to this species and none else. Ladies and gentlemen, boys and girls, I present to you the pied avocet!

A slimly built black-and-white wader—about the size of a blackwinged stilt—but just look at its sleek teardrop-shaped lines! The slinky black-crowned head leads on to a delicate wire-fine, gently upcurving bill that makes the bird look really sophisticated. The snow-white long pointed wings have matching jet-black bars and tips. The tail is shell-white. The delicate legs are greyish-blue. The feet are webbed, and are perhaps the only part of the bird that is not elegant—but don't worry, the bird keeps them mostly out of sight under water! I have always felt that fashion designers need to take a good look at the avocet every morning before beginning their work.

Avocets are chiefly migratory, and visit water bodies in India in winter. They are most commonly found in the north-west parts of the country, less so elsewhere. While they are known to breed in large colonies—of over a thousand pairs—on the Great Rann of Kutch in Gujarat, most of our visitors breed in Central Asia and eastern Europe.

The delicate upcurving bill that makes the bird look so wonderfully snobbish, is actually quite a specialised tool. The

AVOCET

avocet is largely non-vegetarian and runs about on the squelch—or wades tummy deep in the water—wielding its beak at a slanting angle, rather like a hockey stick. It sweeps it from side to side in a semi-circular motion, skimming the surface of the water for minute animal matter. Else, it may upend like a duck, and sweep and search the ooze at the bottom, keeping the two halves of the bill slightly open to snap up aquatic insects, shrimps and even small fish. Often it sweeps its head from side to side, and wades forward briskly through the water. Its webbed feet enable it to swim well whenever it has to.

Avocets are rather wary birds, and if disturbed will fly off swiftly, uttering a loud, clear and high-pitched *klooit-klooit-klooit* call as they go. A flock of these striking pied beauties winging swiftly past, their 'noses' turned up, is an unforgettable sight. In the Rann of Kutch, the birds breed in April, and four eggs are laid in a rough scrape in the ground.

Like Soldiers on the Stones

*A*S THEY STAND STIFFLY TO ATTENTION ON THE HARD stony ground, it is almost impossible to spot them. Clad in sand-brown desert uniforms, these ramrod straight birds do not seem to flick a feather all day. But their enormous goggle eyes, pale gold and baleful, are fixed on you all right. If you do manage to spot one, scan the surroundings carefully—you may well unearth a few more. Some may be squatting under a thorny bush, their legs doubled up under them.

Stone curlews or Eurasian thick-knees as they are now known, are leggy sand-brown birds that stand around 40 centimetres— just over a foot—tall, on long yellow legs which have swollen looking 'knee' joints hence the name 'thick-knees'. The overall plumage is a darkly streaked sand-brown, with a buff coloured bar on the folded wings. The head is thickset, armed with a short stout bill, and studded with a pair of the most enormous golden goggle—or frog-like—eyes. When the birds fly, two white wing bars and a white wing patch on the dark brown wings can help identify them.

They are strange birds indeed. They are 'wading' birds who prefer harsh stony semi-desert areas to squelchy marshes and swamps. Indeed, some have to fly long distances everyday to drink water.

During the day it can get boring looking at stone curlews, because they just stand at their posts like sentries at the gate of an imaginary palace. I see them often at the Delhi zoo—a group of over a dozen birds, and they don't appear to move an inch during the entire two or three hours I might be there! They are not imprisoned and can fly away if they want to.

At the same time, stone curlews are very wary birds. If they find that their camouflage hasn't worked and danger looms, they will take-off swift and low, and fly a short distance before landing and disappearing into the undergrowth. Their retreat into cover is also soldier-like: they slink away furtively in quick darting spurts, necks retracted, heads down—as though under gunfire. Occasionally they'll squat and freeze, their necks laid flat along the ground, great golden eyes fixed on the source of danger.

It is during the evening and night that the stone curlew comes alive and goes hunting. Its huge eyes gives it excellent low-light vision and it snaps up the small creepy crawlies and slinky creatures that come out at this time. Now it utters its plaintive, eerie call, that on full moon nights can make your hair stand on end. It starts off with a string of sharp clear whistling screams. *pick, pick, pick, pick, pick-wick-pick-wick!* or a single penetrating scream, *curliwee!* that may be repeated slowly.

This is also when you might see the bird in the beam of the headlights of your car, if you are motoring down a forest road. It will take a short flight, ahead of you, then land and run a bit, take-off again, run again and so on. In fact, the stone curlew is a 'cursorial' bird—one that is given to running about.

Stone curlews are found throughout the country in dry stony areas and light forests, pebbly river beds, stony hillsides, orchards, groves and even large 'jungly' gardens. They breed between February and August (preferring March and April); two eggs are laid in a scrape in the ground, and incubation lasts for over three weeks.

The males get very aggressive at the start of the breeding season and challenge each other in defense of their territory. They'll stand upright, facing one another, fan out their tails, then stretch and bow and dance threateningly. With the ladies they are more respectful, stretching before them with their necks bowed low, bills almost at their feet.

Many ground nesting birds lose their body scent—or body odour—during the breeding season to protect themselves and their young from predators (such as foxes and jackals) that hunt by scent. It is thought that the stone curlew does something even more: that perhaps it develops a really stinky, pukey, foul body odour at this time to put predators off. Also, its flesh—considered to be delicious at other times—turns bitter and disgusting. So, if man or beast kills and eats one, he'll never try one again in this season. And maybe he will also wake up in the middle of the night, clutch his stomach and utter that eerie desolate scream: *curliwee! curliwee! curliwee!*

'Did-Ye-Do-It?'

I GUESS THAT IF ANY BIRD NEEDED A BODYGUARD IT WOULD be tempted to employ the redwattled lapwing. For this tall (about 30 centimetres or a foot) bronze-brown bird, with its upright stance, alert manner and ringing voice is the first to sense or suspect danger and scream blue murder about it.

The lapwing's most prominent feature is of course, the two blood red wattles it has in front of its dark eyes, which often remind me of huge glistening globules of blood. The bird's plumage is dark bronze brown above, and white below. The head, neck and breast are black. A broad white band runs down from the temple (behind the eye) to the sides of the neck to meet the white undersides. The long legs are lemon yellow, the bill red with a black tip.

The lapwing is a very common bird all over India, and is found in pairs of small groups in open countryside, dry river beds, fields, talao banks, and even forest glades. Usually, it is on a 24-hour red alert and on spotting you (long before you have spotted it) will loudly warn every bird in the area of your evil presence. Now, I did mention that the lapwing might make an excellent bodyguard and sure enough it is extraordinarily alert. But when it sees you, it will flutter aloft and scream penetratingly and accusingly, 'Did-ye-do-it? Did-ye-do-it?' which obviously means it hasn't been able to stop you from doing whatever terrible thing you were planning to do—like perhaps eating its eggs for breakfast! And that means it couldn't really be a very good or effective bodyguard after all. No point screaming after the crime has been committed if your job was to prevent it from being committed in the first place!

Lapwings run about in short brisk spurts, then stop and tilt over without bending their knees, to pick up grubs, insects, seeds, and vegetable matter and suchlike from the ground.

They are noisily watchful at the best of time, but boy do they get hysterical when the breeding season comes around! (They breed between March and August.) Now, if you happen to go even remotely close to the scrape in the ground in which they have deposited their eggs (usually four) both the male and female will flutter around your head like banshees, screaming their lungs out, till the din makes you retreat. They may even dive-bomb you and try the broken wing trick. Actually, they sound so hysterically accusing that even if you haven't the faintest idea where their nest might be, they make you feel as though you had just slaughtered and devoured all their chicks and are now smacking your lips! In the face of these dreadful false accusations, it's better to retreat and let calm return.

Often, I think the birds are terribly foolish. By making such a song and dance, surely they attract attention to themselves and to the fact that there is a nest in the vicinity—possibly with delicious eggs and chicks in it if you are interested in that sort of snack. If the silly birds simply sat tight and quiet, no one would be the wiser about the existence of the nest or eggs. There's no real 'nest' to speak of anyway, and the eggs are so beautifully camouflaged—looking exactly like the clods and rocks around them—that it is virtually impossible to spot them. Even the downy chicks are in camouflage uniform and lie doggo on command. But no! Instead of keeping mum, the adults go and make a hullabaloo and let the whole district know that they've got eggs or a family nearby. Idiots!

It would be interesting to know if indeed, quieter lapwings are more successful in raising chicks to adulthood than the noisier ones, for this reason. If so, it would mean that yes, it is better to remain quiet in the face of danger, than it is to raise hell. But if the noisy ones are more successful, it would mean that attack is still the best form of defence—at least for them—and the bold do better. Actually, I haven't yet met a 'quiet' lapwing, so it does seem as though the screamers are more successful! Possibly, predators like foxes, jackals, mongooses, wild cats and suchlike get completely flustered by this noisy attack and move away quickly for fear of losing an eye to the dive-bombers. So I guess, we'll just have to put up with hysterical accusations of 'Did-ye-do-it? Did-ye-do-it? Did-ye-do-it? Did...did...did!' God! Get me a pair of ear plugs quickly!

The Pinocchio Birds

OF ALL THE BEWILDERING TYPES OF LONG-LEGGED, long-billed, speckled and streaked brown-and-white waders, godwits are amongst the easiest to identify. Simply because they look like Pinocchio would after half-a-dozen good fibs!

Their bills you know, are long—very long. So long that you can't help noticing and pointing. There are two kinds of godwits that spend the winter in India—the blacktailed and the bartailed.

The blacktailed is the larger and more commonly seen of the two, at around 40 to 44 centimetres in length. It is a speckled brown and white bird with a long slender bill, just slightly upturned, and long legs. In flight you'll see a broad white band along the rear (or trailing) edge of the wing as well as a broad black band at the end of the white tail. But you'll have to be quick to notice these when the birds fly, for they are swift and wary. Blacktailed godwits are found in small parties or large flocks (often in the company of other waders) on marshy lakes and tidal mudflats all over the country. Just before they take-off for their breeding grounds in the northern parts of Asia and Europe, their head, neck and breast turn rusty red, as they begin to get into their breeding dress.

Bartailed godwits are similar to, but smaller than, their cousins above and appear to have been fibbing less. Their bills are shorter and more upturned, and their legs too are shorter. When they fly, their legs don't stick out much beyond the tail. They are sandy brown birds, darkly patterned, and don't have the white wing bar, or black and white tail of their cousins. Their tails are narrowly barred in brown and white. Bartailed godwits prefer coastal areas and the northwest parts of the country.

Godwits relish snails, slugs, frog spawn, insects and other squishy creatures living in the mud and ooze. Often, they will wade in belly deep and probe the muddy depths with their heads and bills completely submerged. Truthfully, the stuff must be really delicious!

GODWITS
1. Bar-tailed Godwit, 2. Black-tailed Godwit

Viragos in War Paint

USUALLY IN THE WORLD OF BIRDS, IT IS THE MALES WHO don the war paint and gaudy plumes in their attempt to frighten off rivals and impress the ladies. With the painted snipe, the tables are completely turned: it is the ladies who are all decked up to the eyeballs and bristling with aggro and attitude. Real viragos they are—ladies of strength, courage and stature—and just a little bit overbearing with each other. And as they breed virtually all through the year, they're permanently dressed in their best.

Not that it's easy to spot them—oh, no! The painted snipe lie low in grassy marshes that abound with deep pools and soft muddy patches where you go galumph! guloomph! galooch! if you step in them. But sometimes you can get lucky, as we were one hot Sunday in May at the Sultanpur National Park near Delhi.

Crouching quietly at the edge of a grassy pool were four painted snipe. All ladies. Small squat looking birds, with round

PAINTED SNIPE
1. *Female*, 2. *Male*

heads and long bills. Their metallic olive-green heads were strikingly outlined by a pair of creamish white 'spectacles', and a patch behind the eyes, both of which looked as though they had been carefully painted on by a make-up artist. Similar white bands went over their shoulders rather like the straps of a pair of braces or those of a rucksack. The chin, throat and upper part of the breast were a rich maroony chestnut colour. The lower part of the breast darkened into black, and the undersides were white. All told, they were quite striking as they crouched there by the water like a gathering of warrior queens. Their husbands, who are less showy, didn't seem to be around.

In any case, male painted snipe are quite meek—wimps, really. In this family it is the female who wears the pants. She will fight other females over a gentleman she chooses as a husband. She will warn off other females by spreading open her vividly spotted war-painted wings and bring them forward to meet beyond the tip of her beak, her tail fanned out too. She will hiss and swear at them. She will woo the male with a similar display, showing off her war paint, but hopefully not hiss and swear! Actually, she is said to produce a soft *kok kok* or a long drawn out metallic sounding *oook oook* call while displaying to him; a sound that is apparently like one produced when you blow gently over the mouth of a bottle.

As painted snipe are most active in the early morning, or evening and night, this is when you'll hear them call. All night perhaps, especially if the moon is full.

Once the female has won a husband, she will lay usually four eggs in the rough pad of grass that he has constructed as a nest on the marshy ground. After ensuring that he is safe and well-settled, she walks out on him and goes in search of another husband. The male will quietly incubate the eggs and bring up the chicks.

No, she's not being mean and nasty and doesn't hate babies. You see, for some reason it appears that there are far more gentlemen painted snipe around than ladies. So, it makes sense for the ladies to take on as many husbands as possible and have them bring up the young. She can then lay more eggs—and have more babies—than would have been possible if she had been stuck in a single nest bringing up the young there. And many gentlemen painted snipe would forcibly have had to remain bachelors: This way they are 'married' and usefully employed bringing up the chicks!

Painted snipe are found all over the country, though are not so common in the northwest, central or eastern parts of India. If they sense danger, they prefer running for cover to flying off. They tend to run away in a strangely guilty way—with lowered heads, appearing sheepish. After a while though, they tend to return to the spot (like a criminal returning to the scene of a crime?!) they were flushed from.

The birds feed on molluscs, insects, crabs, worms and suchlike, wagging their rear ends up and down as they do, their long, slightly down-curved (only at the tips) bills probing deeply into the mire. Like in some other waders, the tip of the bill is pitted and sensitive to the movement of these creatures beneath the mud. The painted snipe's eyes are located at the sides of its head and are able to see all around—a full 360°. Which makes it very difficult for you to sneak up unseen on these fabulous viragos in war paint.

Landmine in the Grass

OUT THERE, IN THE SQUELCHY GRASS AT THE EDGE OF the marsh, you tread warily. After each step you pause and scruitinise the area around you thoroughly with your binoculars. Nothing stirs. In the distance, a lapwing screams. You take a few steps, stop and yet again look around you. Nothing.

You relax a bit and put down your glasses.

'There's nothing...'

Bouff! Bouff! Bouff!

The triple muffled explosions come right from your feet and set your heart leaping and kicking like a bucking bronco. You barely see the three brown narrow-winged marsh birds zing away, zig-zagging madly, low over the squelchy marsh grass. Yet again, the common—or fantail—snipe have ambushed you successfully, after lying hidden like landmines in the grass.

You wait till your heart slows to a civilised canter and then proceed in roughly the direction the birds disappeared. But it is only if you are extremely lucky, vigilant and observant that you may be able to spot them because when the snipe crouch in the grass, or even in the open in the mud, they turn virtually invisible.

If your luck is in, you might see a small dark brown wader, streaked and striped with black and buff crouched low, eyeing you warily. Its head is striped like a melon, and its bill is long and straight.

I've always believed that snipe carry a small charge of gunpowder attached to their bottoms, which they set off when danger threatens, sending them zinging off to safety like missiles gone mad. Honestly, they must be able to outrace even a Formula One Ferrari racing car!

Common snipe are migratory birds in most of India and so, will ambush you only between the months of September and April. They do breed in Kashmir and the Himalayas, in May and June, and at this time, the male performs stunning aerobatics to impress the female. He circles high in the sky and then zooms down over her, the wind buzzing loudly through his narrow wing and tail feathers. After the airshow is over, the pair settle down in a shallow grass-lined depression in the ground, where usually four eggs are laid.

Snipe relish worms, insect larvae and other squishy things they find in the mud with their long probing bills.

You might think that the painted snipe we met earlier, and the common snipe we met here are related. After all, they look similar and a snipe is a snipe, right?

Wrong! According to all the bigwig scientists and ornithologists, the common or fantail snipe is a 'true' snipe. The painted snipe is an imposter! Believe it or not, the painted snipe is more closely related to the jacanas and have some features in comon with cranes! Then why on earth do they look so much like these so-called 'true' snipe?

Well, it seems that they took a liking to the 'true' snipe's lifestyle and diet. They liked the same squelchy marshes and muddy jheels; they liked probing deep for slugs and snails and worms and stuff. And so, over the centuries they began to evolve and look like the 'true' snipe. This is called 'convergent evolution'—where two biologically and genetically unrelated species 'converge', or come together, so to speak, and begin to resemble each other because they share the same way of life and environment and diet.

And yes, there's another 'true' snipe you may come across in the marshes in winter. It's called the Jack snipe and is smaller than the common snipe and doesn't have a central stripe over the top of its head. Also, it doesn't carry a charge of gunpowder attached to its bottom so doesn't explode from under your feet. Actually it is quite a sluggish flyer. Well, thank God for small mercies!

A Bit of Shanky Panky!

THE MULTITUDES OF LONG-LEGGED, LONG-BILLED, salt-and-pepper plumaged waders that crowd the banks of the jheels, rivers and other water bodies in winter can drive a birdwatcher crazy. They all look so similar that you can go nuts trying to identify them. Also, it doesn't help much that at this time of the year, they are not dressed in their distinctive breeding finery, but instead, are casually attired in wishy-washy grey and brown patterns.

So, how does one tell a redshank apart in this motley crowd? For a start, it is one of the taller and bigger of the clan, about three-quarters the height of the black winged stilt. Secondly, its narrow straight bill has a red 'racing' stripe zipping out from the base. Thirdly, look for orange-red legs ('shank' is the section between knee and ankle, so the bird has been well-named). Otherwise, it is greyish-brown above, white below, delicately streaked with

brown on the breast. Usually, you will find it by itself or in small groups (with other waders), busy probing for insects and suchlike from the mud. It is an alert bird and will take-off with a shrill piping *tweee tiwee tiwee*! or *tiu, tiu, tiu*! if you disturb it. Now, look for a white border or band on the rear edge (the trailing edge) of its wings, and finely barred white tail. If it's got those, then bingo! you're right on target and redshank it is!

If it hasn't got the white wing bar, but otherwise

1. REDSHANK, 2. GREENSHANK

more-or-less fits the description (and appears a little spotty!), then it's probably the spotted or dusky redshank. Actually its bill is longer and finer than that of the common redshank, but you will need to have them both side by side to make this out. As summer approaches and the birds prepare to leave, spotted or dusky redshanks actually do begin to turn more spotty and dusky!

If the bird you see flying off doesn't have the vital white wing bar and its legs appear to be a dull military green, then worry not! If not the common redshank, or the spotted redshank, it has to be the greenshank naturally! Actually, the greenshank is the largest of the confusing sandpiper clan to visit India, though you can only tell that if you have all of them line up in front of you. Otherwise, it has a slightly upturned bill, and is a dark grayish brown above, and white below. The forehead, rump and lower back are white; the tail faintly barred. And yes, it often keeps company with redshanks.

The redshank breeds in Kashmir and Ladakh, between May and July. Four eggs are laid in a depression hidden in a clump of grass in the middle of squelchy marsh. In summer, the bird is more darkly streaked and marked. The other two are completely migratory.

Pipers in the Mud

ACTUALLY, I WOULD RENAME SANDPIPERS, 'MUDPIPERS' because you find them happily scuttering about in mud and squelch more often than on sand. And yes, they do all 'pipe', or squeak musically, and this is very important when you are trying to identify them because each type of sandpiper has its own particular kind of squeak.

Personally, I've always been confused and confounded by sandpipers because they're all so similar looking. I mean, they're these graceful little grey-brown birds with slender bills and legs, that run around in the mud, picking up insects, molluscs and other stuff, all looking like one another. Their most endearing characteristic is their habit of bobbing their rear ends up and down like one of those funny weighted bend-over toy birdies you can get at fun-fairs. Actually, when real sandpipers do this, it means that they're nervous and about to fly away.

Sandpipers are migratory birds and turn up at water bodies all over the country in winter, some arriving as early as July and some staying on as late as May. At this time their markings are faded and indistinct, their colours pale and wan, which makes it even more difficult to identify them. Still, as birders it is our duty to try and identify at least the more common ones, so here goes. And best of luck when you confront them in the mud!

The common sandpiper is smaller than a partridge, greyish-greenish-brown above with a paler dusky breast. It has a few paintbrush-like dark streaks on the neck. When it zips off, look for a white wing bar and brown tail end. Usually it likes being alone.

The marsh sandpiper is larger, about partridge sized, greyish-brown above with a pure white forehead, eyebrow, temples (the sides of the head) lower back and rump. The underside is also white. The sides of the breast are marked with brown. The bill is black, and straight and thin. The legs are slender and green. There's no wing bar.

The wood or spotted sandpiper is again, smaller than the partridge, pale sepia-brown above, and spotted (though not very distinctly) with white. The breast is pale brownish, the lower back and rump are white. A whitish stripe runs above the eye from the bill to the back (nape) of the neck. This sandpiper likes company.

The green sandpiper is the darkest of the four. It is a stocky bird, dark greenish-brown on top, whitish below. When it flies, the very dark undersides of its wings and the dazzling white belly, rump and vent help identify it. It is shy and solitary.

SANDPIPER
1. Common Sandpiper, 2. Green Sandpiper

Confused by all those vague descriptions of greyish-brown and greenish-brown and greyish-greenish-brown birds? Well, I am! Anyway, let's listen to their calls and see if we can do better. These are what are called their 'flushing' calls, which is what they utter when they are scared away (no, not flushed down the toilet!) by exasperated and frustrated birders trying to identify them!

The common sandpiper emits a shrill piping *tee-tee-tee* as it flees, low over the water with rapid stiff wingbeats. If you can catch one unawares, you might hear it singing sweetly to itself— trilling *wheeit, wheeit* repeatedly again and again.

The marsh sandpiper takes off with a shrill double-noted *chi-weep chi-weep*.

The wood or spotted sandpiper utters a high-pitched *chiff-chiff-chiff* as it zips off.

The green sandpiper has a loud ringing *tluee-tueet*, and *tuee-weet-weet* alarm call.

Happy listening!

Now you see it, Now you don't!

THE LITTLE RINGED PLOVER IS ONE OF THE LARGE exasperating tribe of 'now-you-see-it-now-you-don't!' birds that scuttle about at the edges of ponds and jheels or on vast gleaming mudflats. Your only real chance of spotting one is when it moves, after which you will have to fix your sights on it like a laser-guided missile. But it is such a sweet-looking, dumpy little thing (no, I will not use that ghastly word 'cute'!) that you will instantly forgive it for playing hide and seek with you.

It's about the size of a fat, round chick with a head and bill like that of a pigeon. It has virtually no neck at all which makes it look all the more plump. Its large dark eyes are circled with a neat sunflower yellow ring which makes it look endearingly solemn. It is sandy brown above—usually, the exact shade of the mud it is running about on—and white below. It has a white patch on the forehead, which looks like a hole cut in the broad black mask it wears across its face. It also wears a broad black collar around the base of its throat—all of which give it a very interesting appearance. Its legs are bare and yellow, and the male and female are dressed alike.

Little ringed plovers are resident birds found in pairs or small groups on mudflats, sandy river beaches, talao banks and such places, all over the country. In winter the residents are joined by slightly larger migratory cousins from abroad. They eat tiny creatures like crabs, insects and sand-hoppers found in the mud. They nest between March and May; four eggs are deposited on the bare sand or shingle beach, and merge beautifully with the ground.

I once met a little ringed plover at the edge of a roadside pond near Sambhar lake in Rajasthan. It was scuttling hither and thither in its typical manner—running a short distance in a quick spurt then braking to a sudden standstill and hoping it had disappeared! I found, that by keeping absolutely still myself, I could fool the bird into thinking I was just a part of the scenery and so not dangerous to approach. And so, it scuttled quite close to me without realising I was there. Well, two can play the same hide-and-seek game, I suppose!

The Flicker Flyers

*A*T FIRST IT LOOKED LIKE A HUGE CLOUD OF SMOKE BEING blown swiftly, hither and thither all across the horizon by the wind. But then, as it speedily drew close, magic began to happen. The dark brown cloud vanished for an instant and then suddenly reappeared, flickering silver, and speeding across the sky at breathtaking speed. Then, silver turned back into dark brown, and then back to silver, all the time creating wonderful shifting patterns against the sky. As the magic cloud swooped low over the lake, it began to break up, and now, through the binoculars I could see that it was made up of hundreds of swiftly flying brown birds. When they wheeled and flew away from me, two white 'tail lights' flashed from their rumps, and I could see narrow white bars on their wings. These were the first clues to their identity. At last they landed on the muddy edges of the jheel, and promptly vanished as they came to a standstill.

But I knew they were there, and relentlessly scanned the mud till I found them. Fairly upright standing greyish-brown birds, about partridge-sized but taller, with scaly patterned plumage and a somewhat short bill that looked as though it had been cut to half its proper length. The legs were orange. There were smaller versions too in the crowd. Ruffs and reeves—that's what they were!

This is the only species of bird that I know of (perhaps there are others) where the male and female had different names. The males were known as ruffs, the females, as reeves. Now, I don't know why the females were called reeves, but I do know why the males are called ruffs. (Alas—now both male and female are called ruffs!) In the breeding season, which is summer, the males undergo a spectacular transformation. They put on this huge fluffy, snobbish-looking 'ruff' around their heads and necks and grow fancy ear tufts too, all of which makes them look like very regal lion-birds. Or, if you'd like to poke a bit of fun at them— like those girlish (effeminate is another word for this), curly-haired, over-powdered, lace-wearing noblemen that graced the Royal courts of Britain and Europe when Shakespeare was alive. And this feathery headgear is fantastically coloured in combinations of black, white, purple (a Royal colour!) chestnut and biscuit-brown.

At this time, not only do ruffs look like noblemen, but they try and behave like them too. A large group of noblemen ruffs will gather at specially chosen spots called 'leks'. Each ruff will very grandly defend a few square inches of territory from yon vile knave next door—another ruff doing the same thing a few inches away! The two birds will crouch facing each other, beak pointed downwards, and pompously fluff out their headgear. Then the challenge will be thrown and they'll leap and charge. Usually it's all just for show—to impress the visiting reeves—and no one gets hurt. No real ruff-tuff stuff takes place. The reeves choose who they think are the most handsome and gallant of the noblemen for a husband, and later, move away to a safer place to lay their eggs (usually four). The chivalrous noblemen continue jousting with each other and wooing other ladies. They take no part in family life.

Sadly, we in India don't get to see this wonderful 'tamasha' because the ruff and reeve are migratory birds and only spend the winter here. But one year, in March, while tramping around Sultanpur jheel (near Delhi) I was brought up short by an amazing sight.

Up front, the edge of the lake appeared to be very muddy and clotted—as though a whole heard of cattle had just done a corps de ballet on it. Then suddenly, the whole clotted lake bank appeared to move sideways, just a bit. I blinked and rubbed my eyes. Had I been out in the sun for too long? I went a bit closer and looked through the binoculars. The whole clotted looking lake bank was actually a crowded mass of ruffs, clustered thickly together. Each bird would occasionally lower its head and charge at its neighbour. This made the neighbour back off a bit, or he in turn would lower his head and charge another neighbour. The movement would spread through the flock, making it look as though the whole lake bank was moving. While many of the birds had turned very gingery and orangey around the neck and throat, I was disappointed that none had as yet put on their complete head-dress. A strange guttural muttering emerged from the flock, a sound that indicated a sort of bottled up anger. Probably the birds were only rehearsing for the real performance which would be given on the marshes of northern Asia and Europe later that summer.

The wonderful 'flicker fly' display they put on before landing is also performed by many other birds. A cruising eagle or hawk would find it difficult to single out a target in such a swiftly moving mass of birds. It couldn't risk just diving into the flock at random; a mid-air collision would mean instant death. Also the swiftly changing colours—from brown to silver and back—confuse the raptor further.

Ruffs and reeves can be found on marshy water bodies all over the country in winter, but are more common in the north. They eat insects, minute vegetable matter and algae.

Blizzard Birds

ON THE CREAKING, GENTLY SWAYING PONTOON BRIDGE, we watched the sun come up over the wide, placid Jamuna, glinting peach-gold in the pre-dawn light. Above, the sky was still a dark, midnight blue, but paling fast. Apart from a few hopeful shuffling crows and some mynas there weren't very many birds to be seen. Far away, a squadron of cormorants winged swiftly across the orange-gold sky.

Then a scooter drew up near us, and the rider got off, holding two polythene bags in his hands. And suddenly we were in the midst of a blizzard of raucous and ravenous seagulls who had literally turned up out of thin air! As the man opened the packets and began tossing the savoury snacks out to them, they swirled all around us, deftly grabbing pieces in mid-air and greedily snatching them from one another. They hovered like starving angels right above our heads, their long wings flushed peach-gold and translucent. Some looked as though they wanted to perch on our heads. There must have been five hundred of them whirling around us, and there were others winging their way lankily over the water, on their way to join the feeding frenzy. The air was filled with their hoarse raucous calls and quarrelsome screams, *Keeah! Keeah! Ka-yek! Ka-yek! Kyaaar! Keck! Kuk! Reeah!* Part

GULLS
1. *Blackheaded Gull (Winter), 2. Brownheaded Gull (Summer)*
2a. *Brownheaded Gull (Flight, Winter)*

of the flock soon settled on the water like ducks, stabbing out at each other and gobbling down titbits that came their way. Others were being chased by piratical crows but usually outflew them easily, apparently enjoying the chase.

After the initial flurry, we settled down too, to watch them less breathlessly. The sun was up now, lighting up the birds nicely. Some were pale ash-grey above, with black-tipped white wings, studded with a white 'mirror' near the ends. These were brownheaded gulls.

The others were slightly smaller, about the size of crows, with neater looking heads and no white mirror or black wingtips. The front (leading) edge of their wings glimmered pure white. These were blackheaded gulls. Both had red bills.

Ah, yes, but what about their brown and black heads? Unfortunately, in winter—which is when these birds visit us— the heads of both species turn white. It is only towards the end of March, just before they leave, that their heads begin to turn coffee-brown (a darker shade for the blackheaded), and they begin to look really smart. And where do they go? Well, brownheaded gulls breed in colonies around the high mountain lakes of Ladakh and Tibet. The blackheaded gulls breed further afield in Central Asia and Europe.

In winter, they fly down to our eastern and western coasts and inland waters, frequenting harbours, fishing villages, rivers running through towns, lakes, and so on.

Seagulls are considered to be amongst the most 'successful' of birds in the world, because they are now found in huge flocks nearly everywhere—even in big cities all over the world—and often very very far away from the sea. This is because they have developed a great liking for our trash and will fly miles to scavenge in a good stinking trash dump. In cities like New York for instance, there are enormous flocks of these birds swirling around the gigantic rubbish dumps. Indeed it may just happen that seagulls give up eating fresh fish altogether and live exclusively on left-over or thrown-away cans of sardines and mackarel and tuna and stuff like that! They have become scavengers par excellence, and in a world full of rubbish, well naturally, scavengers will succeed!

Here in Delhi, I make it a point to spend at least one early morning every winter with the gulls that flock to the Jamuna. They have become used to being fed by people like the man on the scooter who said he fed them every morning. I think they fly beautifully—with languid ease and immense grace. And even if they are the world's most successful scavenger and have atrocious table manners, I will still go down to the river and stand in the midst of a seagull blizzard!

About Terns

I USED TO THINK (AND STILL DO) THAT GULLS FLEW beautifully, but that was before I watched terns fly. Slimmer, sleeker and swifter than gulls, terns are like aircraft designed for long-distance racing. They fly with powerful steady wingbeats, and a nonchalant ease, covering large distances in very quick time. Whenever I try to photograph them in flight I'm amazed at how quickly they go past, yet at the same time, they never seem to be in a hurry at all. And they can brake to a standstill in mid-air, and dive missile-like into the water after a fish, in an instant.

And of course, they can do left turns and right turns and 'U' turns and about turns with tremendous ease. They are terns after all, and have to live up to their name!

The trouble with terns in that they can be confoundingly difficult to sort out—especially in winter when our resident

TERNS
1. River tern, 2. Whiskered tern, 3. Black-bellied tern

terns are joined by several migratory ones, which at this time of the year, all end up dressing very much like one another.

Anyway, to keep the confusion to a minimum, I've selected three of our resident species—though they too, will give you an idea of the mix-ups they can cause! The river tern is one such resident. It is about pigeon-sized, but slimmer and can be found flying up and down (as though patrolling) lengths of jheels and rivers all over the country, its gaze directed steadfastly downwards at the water. It is a slim graceful bird, silvery grey and white, with a long deeply forked tail. Its bill is deep yellow and its short stumpy legs are red. In summer its forehead, crown and back (nape) of the neck turn glossy jet black. In winter, the head turns greyish white, marked with streaks of black, especially on the nape.

River terns dive like darts after fish, emerging from the water with their prize held across their sharp bills. The fish is then tossed up and swallowed head-first as the bird continues to fly in its usual relaxed manner.

River terns breed between March and May, laying three eggs on the bare ground on the sandbanks of large broad rivers. They nest together in colonies.

The Indian whiskered tern in winter, is rather like the river tern, being grey on top and white below. However, its tail is only slightly forked and its bill is red, not deep yellow. In summer it too wears a glossy black cap, and in addition develops a jet black belly. It is ashy-grey on top.

This tern breeds in Kashmir and the Gangetic plain between June and September, constructing a circular pad of reeds and rushes on floating aquatic vegetation. Two to three eggs are laid and both parents take care of them and the chicks.

In winter, whiskered terns spread over jheels, marshes, tidal creeks and mudflats all over the country.

The blackbellied tern, like the river tern, also has a deeply forked tail. In summer, like the whiskered tern it too develops a black belly.

Ah, this is getting confusing, isn't it? Like one of those I.Q. tests! Ah, yes—remember now, the blackbellied tern has a deeply forked tail which the whiskered tern does not have, but the river tern does have! And it has a black belly which the river tern does not have, but the whiskered tern does! Sorted that out?

Now to its winter wardrobe... In winter, yes, the blackbellied tern's head turns white, streaked with black, In addition, it has a black patch behind the eye. Its bill is orange— falling nicely and confusingly between the deep yellow bill of the river tern and red bill of the whiskered tern!

Blackbellied terns also like patrolling over large rivers and jheels, in flocks. They like resting together too, and will squat close together all facing the wind (possibly because this helps them take-off instantly and almost vertically). They are found throughout the country and breed in March and April in mixed colonies on sandbanks and islets in rivers. Three or four eggs are laid in a scrape in the ground and both parents incubate the eggs and bring up the young.

As I warned you earlier, a number of other species turn up in winter (looking terribly alike) to confuse you further. Not only that, but many terns only put on their 'adult' costumes after they are one or two years old. In their 'juvenile' attire they can be even more confusing! Well, you can take it as a challenge to try and sort them out with the help of a good bird guide, though I must confess I rarely succeed in doing so myself. I get so engrossed in simply admiring the way they fly and dive that I simply forget to note all those intricate details regarding their heads and tails and bills. Well, I suppose I've had my 'tern' at doing so, now it's yours!

We Three Kings

NO MATTER HOW MANY HUNDRED TIMES YOU HAVE SEEN them before, it is impossible to ignore kingfishers. With their brilliant spark-blue colours and firecracker ways, their gleaming dagger bills and bright black eyes, they compel you to pay proper attention to them every time you spot them. While there are twelve species of kingfishers in India—and around eighty four in the world—here we shall meet three of the most commonly encountered kings...

The small blue kingfisher or common kingfisher is fairly common, though not as common as its name suggests. And what a jewel of a bird it is! Little bigger than a sparrow, it is a brilliant blue kingfisher with silver-blue spangles on its head. Its chin is white, its breast and tummy are fiery russet. It has a neat russet and white steak behind its bright eyes. Its bill is a deadly pointed dagger and its tail is short and stumpy. According to legend, kingfishers were originally rather plain birds. But they were the first to be released from Noah's ark and flew straight towards the setting sun when set free. That's why their underparts became so fiery, while their backs took on the reflected colours of the sky...

I've seen these high-spirited little kings many many times, and one morning, decided to spend some time with a pair I spotted fishing in the lake at the Delhi Zoo. They were both sitting jauntily on a branch overhanging the lake, looking intently at the water, their heads cocked to one side. I focused my binoculars on the bird that was closer to me, admiring its plumage. Actually it looked as though it were moulting, because its feathers were not as brilliant as I'd seen in other kingfishers. Suddenly it vanished and there was a soft 'sploosh'. I lowered the glasses just in time to see the bird land back on a branch nearby, with a small silver fish in its beak, which it promptly began to bash up against the branch. Before I could focus the camera on it, the fish disappeared with a gulp and the kingfisher bobbed its head with apparent satisfaction. I spent about an hour watching the little kings fish, in which time they caught four or five fishes apiece. Several dives were unsuccessful, but none the less exciting to watch. They were too quick for me to follow through the binoculars, and anyway were so close I didn't really need them. Like a spark from a short circuit, the little blue bird would dive headfirst into the green water. After the briefest pause, it would shoot out of the water—with or without its victim—and perch perkily on its lookout branch. If it had been successful, the fish would be bashed up and gulped down.

Later, I read up about the kingfisher's diving technique, as I was interested to know what happened underwater. After the bird has taken aim and dived, it grasps its prey between the mandibles of its bill (no, it doesn't stab it) and then swivels around so that it faces back upwards. The buoyancy of its body carries it upwards, assisted by the beating of its wings, and it emerges like some sea-to-air missile from a submarine. The whole action lasts just one third of a second.

I was hoping that these two little kings would be courting, but it soon seemed clear that they were probably over and done with that. I would have liked to watch the female squat bolt upright on her branch, beak in the air, wings drooping down by her side, shivering with excitement, and squeaking plaintively at the male. The male would gallantly have gone fishing, and then presented her with his wedding gift—a fish which naturally she would eat. Then they would mate and remain partners for life.

Instead of all that romantic stuff, what happened was that a couple of bully-boy crows turned up and began harrassing the kings, who eventually gave up and streaked off with a cheerful enough *chichee! chichee!* squeak of farewell. Little kingfishers are common by steams, rivers, lakes and other water bodies and are always worth spending time with. They breed between November and June, bringing up around five or seven young.

More common than the little king, is the whitethroated or whitebreasted kingfisher. Somewhat larger than a myna, this king is clad in a shiny turquoise and dark blue suit, with a sparkling white chin and throat and centre of the breast, that looks rather like a 'shirt front'. Its head, neck and underparts are

KINGFISHERS
1. Whitethroated kingfisher, 2. Pied kingfisher, 3. Common kingfisher

a velvety chocolate brown and its massive dagger bill, a dangerous pillar-box red. The expression on its face makes it look as though it is smiling wolfishly.

As whitethroated kingfishers relish lizards and insects and mice and even young birds, in addition to fish and frogs and tadpoles, they can be found in places quite far away from water. Telegraph wires are a favourite lookout post for them.

When they fly off from a perch, they explode like a blue firework—cackling loudly—their dark-and-light blue wings dazzling. (Look for a large white patch on the wings.) They nest between January and August in tunnels excavated in earth or mud banks—the traditional home of kingfishers. To dig the tunnel, the birds will first fly full tilt, bill-first at the earth bank one after the other, attempting to prise the packed soil loose. Once this has been done and a toe-hold is gouged out, they perch there and begin to drill with their bills. The legs and feet scoop out the soil, the tail acts as a spade to throw the stuff out of the tunnel. The tunnel may be a metre long, usually sloping upwards (so that water cannot run down it and collect at the end) and widens out at the end into an egg chamber. Four to seven eggs are laid, and both parents share all duties. Whitethroated kingfishers announce their claims to a territory with a loud ringing, *killillill...* call, uttered from some tall exposed perch.

At the Keoladeo National Park, we once came across a whitethroated kingfisher that looked as though it had attempted to drill a hole in a block of granite! Actually, it had probably just flown into a tree, for it lay at the base of the tree, its wings outspread, chin raised upwards, eyes closed. When we picked it up, we realised that it was not dead, just unconscious and probably injured. This presented a problem. Strictly speaking, in a national park you are not supposed to interfere in any way, in the lives of the flora and fauna. Strictly speaking therefore, we were to leave the kingfisher where and as we found it, to be eaten alive by ants or pecked to pieces by a raptor. But it was such a fabulous bird... Surely if we took it to the park authorities they might be able to do something to save it?

We were still arguing about what to do (and I was thinking that if we took it with us, it would be wiser to wrap a handkerchief around that formidable dagger of a bill, just in case...), when the kingfisher took matters into its own hands. It suddenly woke up and with a vigorous whirring of its wings, took off like a blue missile.

The two kingfishers described above may be spectacular to look at but they're nowhere near as spectacular in their method of fishing as is the pied kingfisher. About the same size as the whitethroated, the pied kingfisher is dressed in a speckled and barred black-and-white (or well, pied!) suit, and has a short raffish crest. The male wears a double black necklace—or gorget—across the breast, the female has a single, somewhat broken up one.

The pied kingfisher will come streaking over a large water body, gazing intently down at the water as it speeds across. Then, suddenly, it will climb a little higher, till perhaps 30 metres up, and literally, park itself vertically up there in mid-air, its wings beating rapidly, its tail flared open. Hovering thus, its black dagger of a bill pointing straight down, it will scan the water keenly, and then fold its wings and dive. It enters the water like a small speeding arrowhead, emerging successfully, a few seconds later, with a fish clamped in its bill. At other times it will find another spot and will 'stand' on its tail and wait in mid-air again...

What is amazing is that the kingfisher is successful at all. While aiming, it has to take into account that due to the 'bending' or refraction of light as it enters water, the fish will not be where it appears to be, from 30 metres above. (Dip a straw into a glass of water and note how it seems to be 'broken' when it enters the water; this again is due to 'refraction'.) It therefore must correct its aim before hurling down at the fish. Like other kingfishers and diving birds (and in fact, many other animals), the pied kingfisher has a special membrane—like a piece of tracing paper—that protects its eyes just before it enters the water. The membrane, like a translucent third eyelid, stretches across the eye just before impact with the water. It is called the nictitating membrane, and I remember once, watching a whitethroated kingfisher sitting in the sun in the Keoladeo National Park, with the membrane stretched across its eyes like a screen. At first I wondered whether the bird had gone blind, but then I saw the membrane slip down across the eye like a shutter, revealing the sparkling dark pupil behind it.

Sometimes of course, the pied kingfisher fishes like other kingfishers, waiting on a branch overhanging the water and diving straight down after any fish it spots.

Pied kingfishers nest between October and May, raising five or six chicks. If you ever hear a sharp cheery *chirruk! chirruk!*

while near a large pond or tank or water body, turn your back
to the wind and look above the water carefully. Somewhere high
above, you may see this valiant black and white bird hanging
in the sky, all set for a bit of spear fishing.

Air Raiders

THE FOLLOWING FOUR BIRDS ARE NOT 'WATER BIRDS' OR 'waders' in the sense that they live on the water like ducks, or wade about on the muddy banks of jheels, rivers and other water bodies digging in the mud with their bills, like the sandpipers. They are hunters—air-raiding raptors—who prey on waterfowl, waders and shorebirds, as well as on fish and other creatures living in and around such water bodies. They belong to the great fierce family of raptors—the birds of prey—though most of them are not entirely the great and noble birds they are so often made out to be. They are however, wonderful to watch.

Of the four air-raiders we shall meet here, the brahminy kite is certainly the most timid of the lot. Indeed, it is often itself a victim of other air-robbers and pirates like crows and pariah kites and eagles. It is a handsome bird, a little smaller than a pariah kite, with a white head, throat and breast and fiery ginger upper parts. Its call—a harsh squealing—has been described as that of a pariah kite with a sore throat!

Brahminy kites are found all over India, but always near water. They wheel and circle over fishing villages, harbours on the coast, rivers, jheels, and even flooded paddyfields. During the rains they move inland from the coasts, over flooded plains where there are land crabs and frogs to feast upon. Apart from these, and fish, they also eat small snakes, bats and scraps of garbage floating on the water. They breed between December and April and build large untidy platform-like nests high up on large trees, usually near water. Normally, two eggs are laid and both parents incubate them, and bring up the chicks.

No bird has been better named than the marsh harrier. For one, it is almost always found over marshes and swamps and reed fringed jheels. And secondly, if you don't know the meaning of the word 'to harry' (from which it gets its name, harrier—one who harries) just watch the marsh harrier and you'll be left in no doubt as to what the word means!

But first of course, you have to recognise it and be warned— the male and female are so different that it is surprising that even they can recognise one another as their own kind. The female marsh harrier, slightly smaller than a pariah kite, is a dark chocolate brown all over. But on her head she wears a pale cream monkey-cap—like the hood or stocking or balaclava of a bank-robbing bandit. She also has two matching cream patches on her shoulders, which look like epaulettes.

Her husband is a slimmer, sleeker-looking bird, dark rufous brown, with a pale rufous brown head, neck and breast. His long slim wings are silvery-grey, tipped with black, and his tail is also silvery-grey.

Marsh harriers are migratory birds, and follow the vast flocks of waterfowl that make their way over to the Indian subcontinent in winter. They fly in loose causal flocks, and spread out over the marshes and jheels where they know the waterfowl have sought sanctuary.

1. BRAHMINY KITE, 2. MARSH HARRIER
3. OSPREY, 4. PALLAS'S FISH EAGLE

Here they begin their campaign of harassment and terror. As the ducks and coot murmur contentedly in the buttery winter sun, the marsh harrier launches a raid. There is nothing spectacular or breathtaking about it except for the effect it has on the waterfowl. Lazily and languidly, the harrier flies low over the water, examining the panic-stricken waterfowl below as though choosing apples from a fruit stall. As its deadly shadow slips across them, the ducks and coot panic completely. With a desperate flailing of wings and frantic paddling of feet they take to the air together with a clamarous splashy roar. The fear spreads like wildfire across the entire lake, and soon the sky is filled with hundreds of agitated birds wheeling around in blind panic. Undeterred by the great roar of wings, the harrier continues its low relaxed patrol, its eyes sharp on the birds still on the water. And... is that a straggler down there, hiding by the reeds? A weakling, or a sick or injured bird? Braking in mid-air the harrier drops down on its hapless victim.

If it doesn't find one immediately, it will continue to harass and hound and harry the waterfowl until it does. Relentlessly and without let up. And all in that nonchalant, no big deal manner, as though it were on a causal Sunday afternoon flight, and not a deadly hunt. Surely no bird has given a greater number of waterfowl a collective heart attack more often, than has this hooded bandit bird!

Apart from sick and injured waterfowl, marsh harriers also hunt and eat, frogs, fish, small animals and carrion. They like spending hours perched on the ground, or soaring high in the heavens, the wings held in a shallow 'V' well above the body.

If you are ever at a jheel or marsh during winter, and suddenly hear a commotion over the water as two thousand ducks try to take-off at the same time—you can be sure that somewhere in their midst, this bandit will be cruising casually, its eyes glittering coldly behind its monkey-cap hood.

The Pallass's fish eagle or Ringtailed fish eagle is certainly the most powerful of the four raptors we shall meet here. A tall handsome eagle, larger than the parish kite, it is dark brown all over. But, its head is pale golden brown, blond you could say, and across its tail, it has a broad white band which is most visible when it flies.

I've met these regal looking eagles several times—at the Keoladeo and Corbett National Parks—but invariably they just remained perched like stuffy statues on bare tree-tops, looking handsome all right but doing nothing. Once, at the Keoladeo, I heard one call, and first thought that someone had smacked a puppy nearby! *Yelp, yelp yelp!* from such a haughty, regal looking bird!

This eagle is a resident of jheels, rivers and large water bodies in the northern and eastern parts of the country. As a pirate and nest-robber it has made quite a name for itself. It will pounce on other smaller raptors, like kites and harriers and rob them of their rightful prey. It plays havoc with the young of darters and storks and ibises during the monsoons, visiting their nesting colonies with the casual attitude of someone visiting a supermarket. Of course, the poor parents of the young birds get hysterical, and the darters all aim their spear bills at the flying killer, winging so scornfully in their midst. Needless to say, the eagle does well for itself. In winter, it turns its attention to those poor silly coots. One nasty trick is to single out a bird and to continue to pounce on it till it is exhausted by its attempts to escape. Sometimes a pair of eagles join forces to do this. Else, it might simply sit on top of the hapless bird and attempt to drown it. The eagle also pounces on fish swimming near the surface, grabbing at it with its talons, and will also eat rats, snakes, crabs and carrion.

Pallass's fish eagles breed between November and March, building huge structures out of twigs on the tops of large trees. Three eggs are laid and both parents share all the chick-rearing duties.

One would think that such a dacoit of a bird would do well for itself, but it appears that crime does not pay after all: the Pallass's fish eagle is getting quite rare and has been put on the list of birds that are 'globally threatened'. Actually of course, it has nothing to do with their 'criminal' tendencies; probably we, with our pesticides and fertilisers and destructive habits are to blame for their decline.

Another bird that did indeed nearly become extinct in the West due to the use of pesticides—especially DDT (now banned)—is the osprey. This purely fish-eating raptor is a dark brown, long-winged bird with a brown-and-white head. Across the upper part of its dazzling white breast, it has a brown band which looks a bit like a necklace. Its underparts are pure white.

The osprey is a winter visitor to large jheels and rivers, and the sea coasts all over India. It is a long and lean-looking hawk who flies up and down over the water with shallow strokes of its long narrow wings; pausing every now and then for a long glide. A brown band behind the yellow ringed eyes makes it look as though it were wearing a mask.

While I have seen ospreys patrol up and down a length of water, I haven't been lucky enough to watch one fish. If it does happen to spot a fish that has come up to the surface, it may brake to a standstill, and hover awhile, legs dangling, talons at the ready. Then down it plunges, and with a great splash is upon the fish, its talons digging deep. Sometime the fish is strong and heavy and fights back, trying to free itself or drag the bird underwater. And sometimes it succeeds. More often however, the bird wins, rising into the air with effort, the fish dying in its pincer grip. It is taken to a favourite rock and pulled to pieces and consumed. Occasionally, the fish is too heavy to be lifted clear of the water and is dragged across the surface to the shore where it is killed and eaten.

Ospreys breed in the Himalayas, Kashmir, northern Uttar Pradesh and the Northeast, between March and April. A huge untidy nest of large twigs is built on top of a tree on or near water. Two or three eggs are laid and both parents (who look alike, though the female is a little larger) bring up the chicks.

The introduction of DDT into the food chain resulted in the birds (including other species of raptors) laying eggs with very thin shells, that invariably broke, or those that didn't hatch at all. The poor osprey was nearly wiped out because of this, though

now the banning of DDT (and other pestcides) has enabled this magnificent fisherman to make something of a comeback. Unfortunately, many harmful pesticides are still being used in India, and very recklessly indeed, putting the future survival of many birds at risk.